A MOST SECRET SQUADRON

A MOST SECRET SQUADRON

*The First Full Story of 618 Squadron
and its Special Detachment
Anti-U-Boat Mosquitos*

Des Curtis DFC

Grub Street • London

Originally published in 1995 by Skitten Books, Wimborne, Dorset

This edition first published in 2009 by
Grub Street Publishing
4 Rainham Close
London
SW11 6SS

Reprinted 2019

British Library Cataloguing in Publication Data
Curtis, Des.

A most secret squadron : the first full story of 618
Squadron and its special detachment anti-U-Boat Mosquitos.
   1. Great Britain. Royal Air Force. Squadron, No. 618 – History.
   2. World War, 1939-1945 – Aerial operations, British.
   3. Mosquito (Military aircraft) – History.
   4. World War, 1939-1945 – Regimental histories – Great Britain.
   I. Title
   940.5'44'941-dc22

ISBN-13: 9781906502515

Printed and bound in India by Replika Press Pvt. Ltd.

Grub Street uses only Forest Stewardship Council (FSC) paper for its books.

"I must tell you that each of you has been specially selected to join this squadron, and that the particular operation for which we are now training is going to be dangerous, with possibly heavy losses. So, if any of you feel that you would not want to be part of this, you are free to say so now. So, if you want to opt out, please step forward. I promise you that you will be returned to the squadron from which you came, without any stain on your records whatsoever".
– *Wg Cdr G. B. Hutchinson,* DFC

This book is dedicated to all those men who stood fast, and to all the other men and women who served in 618 Squadron and 618 Squadron Special Detachment, Coastal Command

The author in June 1944.

Contents

Appreciation

The major part of this book relates to the plans to mount, at short notice, a low-level daylight attack on the German battleship *Tirpitz* using Mosquito aircraft and the 'bouncing bomb'. This plan was fraught with difficulties, not least because of the distance of the target, but for the need for absolute secrecy. The author has successfully brought together, in an easily understood style, the complex considerations, at very senior level, of mounting this operation with an unproven weapon, and the constricted atmosphere within which aircrew made their preparations.

Plans to attack the *Tirpitz* with the 'bouncing bomb' were finally abandoned and a detachment of 618 Squadron then undertook anti U-boat and anti-surface vessel activities. Their specialist use of a 57 mm gun is a story in itself – and compensated greatly for the frustrations and disappointments of the earlier aborted plans.

A well researched, very readable and well presented book that demonstrates the use of crews with unique training in Mosquito handling and Coastal Command skills.

Air Marshal Sir Ivor Broom
KCB, DSO, DFC, AFC

Foreword

The whole world knows of the daring exploits of No. 617 (Lancaster) Squadron of RAF Bomber Command, when they bombed the Ruhr dams on the night of 16th/17th May 1943. The pundits and military historians will continue for decades to argue whether or not that bombing was successful in military and economic terms.

Little was known of a squadron that was formed within Coastal Command within a few days of the formation of 617 Squadron, that would be using the same principle of weaponry in the Mosquito aircraft. Its secrets remained out of the public domain for many years after the ending of the Second World War.

This book, whose author was one of the founder members of that squadron, attempts to recount the story of No. 618 Squadron, as seen both at the level of the Chiefs of Staff in their planning of the war effort, and from the viewpoint of the pilots and observers who were selected to make up the complement of crews.

Coastal Command was, at all times, closely allied to the Royal Navy, and the Royal Navy were the higher authority when it came to the selection of individual marine targets. The only time in this history when the Royal Navy attempted to 'pull rank' was in its assertion that the Fleet Air Arm should be the first squadron to fly twin-engined Mosquitos from an aircraft carrier. No. 618 Squadron won the day, thanks to the clear decision of Sir Charles (later Lord) Portal, the Chief of Air Staff.

When the Bristol Beaufighter two-seater aircraft was introduced into Coastal Command the second member of the crew had to navigate, operate the wireless and D/F equipment, take aerial photographs and occasionally use the Vickers machine gun to defend the aircraft. That person was categorised as an "Observer/WT" – a name that carried over from the early days of the RFC. The flying brevet was a letter "O" attached to a single wing; NCO Observers wore the 'Lightning Flash' badge of a wireless operator above the chevrons on the sleeve. Individuals who had completed the extra training to qualify as "Observers/WT" were very proud of that aircrew category.

No 618 Squadron was formed with crews from both Coastal and Bomber Commands. The crews from Bomber Command were referred to as Pilots and Navigators. In 1944 Air Ministry instructed that the aircrew category 'Observer' would be discontinued and Observers would then be known as Navigators, wearing a half-brevet with the letter 'N' within laurel leaves. Most of 618 Observers chose to disregard this change of status, however. Air Ministry itself continued to refer to 'Observers' in the August 1945 edition of Pilot's Notes for the Mosquito Mk XVIII, which was flown by some of the 618 Squadron crews.

But, in this book, the 'Observer' or 'Navigator', as the second man in the 618 Squadron Mosquitos, have the same meaning.

The highly secret nature of the squadron resulted in some of the normal squadron records being incomplete. This was particularly true of some of the operations involving 618 Squadron Special Detachment, when no mention of the names of its aircrew was made by the squadron to which it was attached. The author has attempted to fill as many of those gaps as possible.

Each crew member was personally selected to serve with the squadron. They were not just the "usual ration of Pilot Officer Prunes", as the Commander-in-Chief, Coastal Command so aptly remarked.

Some references have been made of the exploits of some of them either before joining 618 or after leaving it. This is not to denigrate in any way the skills, boldness and bravery of others who have not been so mentioned.

Acknowledgements

The author gratefully acknowledges the assistance given, principally by that most efficient establishment, the Public Records Office, Kew. Material included in this book from that source is Crown copyright and is reproduced with the permission of the Controller of Her Majesty's Stationery Office. The Trustees of the Imperial War Museum provided the photographs of the German warships in Altenfjord, Norway. Brooklands Museum, Weybridge, provided some interesting photographs of some of the trials in which the Mosquito aircraft of 618 Squadron were involved. The Royal Air Force Museum provided a photograph.

My thanks also to Leon Murray for his patience in reading the first manuscript and for his helpful comments and suggestions; to Doug Turner, Jimmy Hoyle and Aubrey Hilliard for access to their personal memorabilia. Others who have provided information include Frank Gee, Malcolm Holmes, and Tim Murray in Vancouver, to all of whom I am also grateful.

WZ Bilddienst of Wilhelmshaven provided a photograph of the *Tirpitz*.

Herr Gunther Heinrich provided photographs of U-960 and a personal tour of U-995, and Herr Raimund Tiesler has provided the log of U-976 and photographs of the survivors coming ashore. The French underwater search team, G.R.E.M., provided the picture of the U-boat wreck, and other material. I am greatly obliged to all these people and organisations.

My son, Peter, has given a great deal of support in preparing the work for publication.

DES CURTIS

CHAPTER I
The Battle of the Atlantic

Some historians have referred to the Battle of the Atlantic as one of the greatest battles in history. Certainly that battle was critical for the future freedom of the peoples of Europe – and the battle was fought over a vast area of sea from the Arctic down into the South Atlantic and onto the coasts of the Americas and Africa.

Germany had been restricted by the League of Nations in the extent to which it could re-arm after the First World War, but despite this, Hitler's promises to restore national pride were readily transposed into an immense building programme of submarines and capital ships. In consequence, the German navy was well equipped with modern vessels when the Second World War broke out.

The limitation on the size of surface warships was overcome by designing what came to be called "pocket battleships" and heavy cruisers. Names such as *Lutzow, Admiral Graf Spee, Tirpitz, Scharnhorst, Gneisenau, Admiral Scheer, Prince Eugen,* and *Graf Zeppelin* have entered the annals of naval history. Each was capable of steaming at high speed, with a long cruising range, and its guns were powerful enough for the ship to stand-off from its targets. These ships without smaller escorts could therefore range over the whole of the Atlantic – picking off targets and escaping again into the grey seas.

Admiral Doenitz, a young but experienced U-boat commander of the First World War (he was only 47 at the outbreak of the Second World War), was in command of the U-boat fleet. It is said that he told Hitler in 1939 that, if he had a fleet of 300 U-boats at his disposal, he could starve the British into submission.

As if proof of Germany's naval strength was needed, a U-boat sank the liner Athenia on 4th September 1939 – only hours after war was declared. That was followed 23 days later by the sinking of HMS *Courageous.* But, much more dramatically, a U-boat penetrated the defences of the Royal Navy base at Scapa Flow, in the Orkneys, and sank HMS *Royal Oak* with the loss of 810 lives.

The *Admiral Graf Spee* had been detected by the Royal Navy while it was attacking some of the stragglers of a convoy, and a long chase ensued. The chase ended in triumph for the Royal Navy, as the German ship was finally forced to fight a close battle with HM Ships *Exeter*, *Achilles* and *Ajax* in the South Atlantic. The *Admiral Graf Spee* was mortally damaged off the mouth of the River Plate, near Montevideo and, with no possibility of making it back to a Nazi-friendly port, the ship was scuttled on 11th December 1939.

The fall of France on 25th June 1940 gave the Germans ready access to the Atlantic coast ports such as St. Nazaire, Lorient and La Rochelle, which considerably shortened the time that their U-boats spent away from their hunting grounds. The hard pressed British and Commonwealth navies could not deploy all their resources to U-boat hunting, as that would have meant turning their backs on the pocket battleships that were also causing havoc amongst the merchantmen. In November 1940, the *Admiral Scheer* sunk HMS *Jervis Bay* while it was defending a convoy. Some idea of the scale of the battle can be gleaned from the frightening statistic of over half a million tons of shipping having been sunk each month during the second half of 1940 and first months of 1941; that was way outside the ability of the shipyards to provide replacement tonnage.

By the beginning of 1941 Britain and her empire stood alone against the might of the German forces; the British Empire was making men and materials available to resist the enemy thousands of miles away in Europe. Within the British Isles, the population of civilians and service people, their numbers swollen both by the refugees from Continental Europe and by the servicemen from Canada, Australia, South Africa and elsewhere, would not be able to survive for more than days without substantial seaborne imports of food and raw materials.

One important factor that helped save the day – and there were to be several others – was the willingness of neutral countries to offer their ships to the Allies and for crews to still be coming forward to man these ships in spite of the enormous losses of seamen, which could not be concealed.

Many of the pre-war liners, such as the Queen Elizabeth, those in the Union-Castle Line, the New Zealand Shipping Company, etc were capable of maintaining good cruising speeds, and were permitted to travel alone without naval escort. Other Allied shipping was obliged to travel in convoy to make most use of mutual defence

and of the available naval escorts. Some merchantmen in those convoys were equippped on the poop-deck with a gun to add to the
defences against a visible U-boat. The convoys were segregated into
those which could maintain a mimumum set speed and those which
would be slower. Sometimes it was necessary to merge both types of
convoy, and the whole convoy had to slow down. For the sake of the
majority, ships that suffered mechanical failure or were forced by
enemy action to reduce speed had to be left to their own devices. For
the convoy to stop to pick up survivors would offer sitting targets to
the hunters, so survivors had to rely on being recovered by the escort
vessels.

On 6th April 1941 the *Gneisenau* was badly damaged near Brest by
a torpedo from an RAF aircraft. Later, in February 1942, she and her
sister-ship, the *Scharnhorst*, together with the cruiser *Prinz Eugen,*
made a succeessful dash through the English Channel in fog. They
had been ordered to stand-by to repel a possible second Allied landing in Norway. The *Prinz Eugen* was torpedoed by a Britsh submarine a few days later and put out of action. The *Scharnhorst* was
sunk by the Royal Navy in the Battle of North Cape in December
1943.

The *Bismarck* was sunk on 27th May 1941 but sadly, only three
days earlier, HMS *Hood* was lost. The month of November 1941 was
disastrous, as on the 14th, HMS *Ark Royal* was lost, then in the space
of two days, HMS *Dunedin* and HMS *Barham* were sunk.

When France capitulated the French naval squadron at Oran in
Algeria was ordered to immobilise its vessels – so denying the Allies
of a chance to supplement their resources. Later, in November 1942,
when the Germans entered the city of Toulon, Admiral Darlan
ordered the French naval commanders there to scuttle all the ships.
Once more, valuable resources to use against the Germans were
denied to Britain. (Admiral Darlan was assassinated on Christmas
Eve of that year). The Italian fleet had been attacked by the Fleet Air
Arm at Taranto, so reducing the threat from that quarter.

Every loss of a British naval vessel left the convoys more exposed
than ever, and it seemed that Admiral Doenitz was going to succeed.

The German Navy were using long-range Focke-Wolfe FW-200
Condor reconnaissance/bomber aircraft to patrol far out into the
Atlantic, seeking out convoys and Allied naval units. The information gained enabled the High Command to issue fresh interception
instructions to its surface vessels and U-boats. Nearer in to the coasts,

the German anti-shipping bombers were the Heinkel HE-111 and the Dornier 217. The *Kriegsmarine* under Admiral Doenitz had developed the technique of hunting in packs of U-boats. A reconnaissance Folke-Wolfe Condor or a watching U-boat would detect the presence of a convoy – often by the smoke from the funnels on the horizon before the ships were sighted. The U-boats would maintain watch during daylight and, when the U-boat pack had taken up positions, move in to the attack during the hours of darkness. The harassment of a convoy would sometime go on for days on end, with appalling losses.

The United States entered the war after the Japanese attack on Pearl Harbour in December 1941. This meant that US warships, ceasing to be neutral, could be added to the resources pitted against the U-boats. The Gulf of Mexico and the Caribbean were areas where the U-boats were preying on the tankers bringing oil from Venezuela to the United States and to England and other free countries.

In 1940 and 41 most of the shipping losses were in mid-Atlantic and in Northern waters bordering the Arctic Circle. There was a noticeable shift in the pattern of losses in the first six months of 1942, when most of the shipping losses were off the US East Coast, in the Gulf of Mexico, and off South Africa – usually close in to the shore. This apparent contradiction can be explained by the fact that, although American was by then at war with Germany, rigid and mandatory black-outs of cities and towns had not been imposed on the coastal areas. In consequence, the merchant ships and tankers were offering perfect silhouettes for the U-boat packs, positioned on the seaward side.

But what of the Allies fighting power in the skies over the Atlantic? In the early days of the war, the Fleet Air Arm was equipped with that brilliant but old Swordfish aircraft, and some amphibians – but the flying ranges of ship-borne aircraft was very limited. Some merchant ships were modified to allow Hurricanes to be catapulted off, but of course, landing on and operating in heavy seas restricted their use. They could at least offer some protection against the enemy bombers, such as the Condors.

The battle of the skies around Britain had been won in the Battle of Britain, and the air offensive was being mounted against Occupied Europe and in support of our ground forces in North Africa. There were precious few aircraft – of the right type – to make any substantial impact on the battle for the control of the seas.

Royal Air Force Coastal Command had, in the early days of the war, been something of a cinderella branch of the service. For example, in June 1940 the only aircraft under its command that were capable of operating beyond a 500 mile radius were 34 Sunderland flying boats. Its other aircraft, such as Lockheed Hudsons, Bristol Blenheims, Beauforts and later Beaufighters gave a good account of themselves both in intercepting the German aircraft en route to and from the convoys, and in attacking German shipping moving along the coasts of Norway, Denmark, Holland, Germany and France. One important German route was that which brought Swedish and Norwegian iron ore to the foundries and plants in Germany.

But more long-range aircraft to provide air cover for the convoys in mid-Atlantic, better means of detecting U-boats than relying solely on visual contacts or message flashed by convoy escorts, and specialised depth-charges to carry out an attack in place of the general purpose bombs that were standard equipment initially were all desperately needed. Help was not far away – and things were going to improve pretty quickly.

The British Isles had long ceased to be self-sufficient in food, and, of course, other materials such as oil were vital to keep the nation alive and able to fight back. Food could not be brought the short distance across the English Channel, so the success of the convoys in reaching Britain was key to survival or submission. Rationing had been introduced very quickly, but by 1941 the already meagre ration of food was having to be cut further. For a nation of tea drinkers, two ounces of tea per week per person made the tea leaf a precious commodity. There was no point in exhorting the nation to "Go to Work on an Egg" when only one egg per person per fortnight was allowed. 1941 fell behind to make way for 1942 with no real improvement in this plight.

Prime Minister Winston Churchill and President Franklin Roosevelt met at Casablanca in January 1943 and declared that the top priority must be given to winning the war against the U-boats; in every way, from the design room of the shipyards where new U-boats keels were being laid down every week to the deepest seas where that enemy might be lurking.

In March 1943 Fast Convoy HX 229 caught up with Slow Convoy SL 122, making a new group of 90 merchant ships and 16 escorts. They had been shadowed by a pack of 38 U-boats, which succeeded in sinking 21 of those 90 ships.

In that month alone, the Allies lost more than 500,000 tons of merchant shipping; by contrast, one U-boat was sunk. It was known that in April the Germans had 240 serviceable U-boats. But – in May – less than two months after those disastrous losses, 31 U-boats were sunk.

Some of the means by which the Allies were going to defeat the U-boats are well known and documented.

The most significant development was the way that the Allies were able to turn to their advantage the Enigma coding system. How this machine came to be in Allied hands, and how its immensely complicated encoding system was cracked is a powerful story in its own right – but there were two vital consequences. Firstly, the German naval codes became known and thus it was possible for the Allied commanders to receive German intelligence and orders as soon as they were known to the German officers in the U-boat packs and in the pocket battleships. Secondly, and almost unbelievably, the fact that the German Enigma codes had been compromised was kept secret not only during the remainder of the war but throughout the next two decades. Elaborate communication systems were devised to relay information derived from Enigma only to those who had a need to know, and those communication systems certainly worked to good effect.

Another important development in so far as the individual U-boat commander was concerned was the rapid development and deployment of airborne radar, known as ASV (Air to Surface Vessel). A young British scientist, Alan Dower Blumlein, had been pioneering stereo sound and high definition television for EMI; he was seconded to work under Sir Bernard Lovell at the Government Research Establishment at Malvern. Early in 1942 his team had come up with a radar system which was able to display the important features of the ground beneath the installation; H2S was the name given to this system, which was operational for the first time in January 1943. Bomber Command wanted the full production but, following the priority dictated at Casablanca, the Admiralty succeeded in persuading the War Cabinet to instal the first sets into anti U-boat aircraft. 29 sets were allocated to Coastal Command as "ASV", and were fitted into Vickers Wellington twin-engined bombers. Coastal Command aircrew were given rapid training in the use of the equipment, and early in 1943 spectacular results were achieved.

Until then the U-boats had been able to operate in packs knowing that their enemies – the convoy escort vessels – had to rely mostly on sonar responses to locate them; they knew also that Allied aircraft had to see them before an attack could take place. Then, suddenly, that all changed. In daylight or darkness, the ASV Mk 111 Radar was able to home in on a hull and even a periscope. The Wellingtons, and the Liberators, which had also been introduced to close the Atlantic gap, played havoc with the U-boat packs. Sadly, Alan Blumlein and five of his scientific experts perished on 7th June 1942 when the Halifax bomber, in which they were testing radar equipment, mysteriously crashed in flames over the Wye Valley. His contribution to the battle was so significant that Winston Churchill ordered that his death should be kept secret, to deny the Germans the knowledge that this brilliant mind had been lost.

A third, but perhaps less spectacular, piece of equipment that was brought into use around this time, again fitted to Vickers Wellingtons initially, was the Leigh Light. Sqn Ldr Leigh, working in Coastal Command, came up with the practical idea of removing the front turret of a Wellington bomber, and replacing it with a searchlight. Then, while flying at a comfortably low altitude, as soon as a surface contact was established, the light would be switched on – to both dazzle any U-boat crew on deck, and to light up the target onto which depth charges would then be dropped. This was a far more precise way of illuminating such a target than by the use of magnesium flares.

The enormous value of ASV and the Leigh Light was demonstrated later in the war. On 8th June 1944, a Liberator of 224 Squadron, with Flg Off K.O. Moore in command, flying at 500 feet, made an ASV radar contact 12 miles dead ahead. Using the moonpath, the crew sighted a fully surfaced Type VII C U-boat. The Leigh Light was not used, and at 02.15 hrs a low level attack was made with 6 depth charges. Less than half an hour later, another U-boat contact was made, and a similar attack from 50 feet with 6 depth charges was made. That U-boat was seen to sink, and the Leigh Light was turned on to help survivors struggling in the water to get to the three dinghies which had been launched before the boat sunk. U-629 and U-373 were lost, while patrolling the approaches to the

English Channel in the first days of the Normandy landings – all in the space of half an hour!

The Type VII C U-boat was not then fitted with the schnorkel breathing device, so they were obliged to spend some of the dark hours on the surface, recharging batteries and changing the air in the hull. This improved the prospects of being detected by radar. Admiral Doenitz, in his memoirs, writes that "The U-boats were robbed by radar location of their fighting power. We had lost the battle of the Atlantic". Winston Churchill described in a speech to the House of Commons how "Long lines of U-boats were spread to intercept these convoys, and packs of fifteen to twenty U-boats were often concentrated upon the attempt. To meet this British, American and Canadian forces of the sea and air hurled their strength upon the U-boats. The fighting took place mainly around the convoys, but also over wide expanses of the ocean. It ended in the total defeat of the U-boat attack." That total defeat was not to come until the last days of the war in Europe.

There were other scientific brains working on novel ideas to cripple Germany's naval might. One of the weapons that was invented and developed was once described by Air Officer Commanding-in-Chief, Bomber Command, Air Marshall Sir Arthur Harris, as "just about the maddest proposition as a weapon that we have yet come across and that is saying something".[1]

---

[1] Letter from Sir Arthur Harris to Air Chief Marshal Sir Charles Portal dated 18th Feb. 1943: Source: Public Record Office (PRO) AIR 6-63

CHAPTER 2

Dr. Barnes Wallis and Weapon Developments

The man about whom "Bomber" Harris had been somewhat scathing was Dr. Barnes Wallis, who would, in later years, be knighted by Her Majesty in recognition of his services to the country.

Barnes Neville Wallis was born in 1887, and after serving an apprenticeship in marine engineering, he became a draughtsman with Vickers Airships, before the outbreak of the First World War. During that war he was in charge of airship production at Vickers, Barrow-in-Furness. It is probable that it was during that time that he developed what would be a lifelong interest in long distance travel.

Vickers were working after the war on an airship design, the R80, but the Government lost interest in the project and Barnes Wallis was laid off by Vickers. He put his time to good use, by first obtaining a degree in engineering, then teaching maths in Switzerland.

Government in the mid-20's put up the idea of an Empire Communications Scheme, based on airships. At that time, the only means of communication across the oceans were by wireless telegraphy or ship-borne mail. Vickers Armstrong offered Barnes Wallis re-employment, this time as Chief Designer of its R100 airship. A great deal of public interest had been aroused by the flight of a German airship across the Atlantic with 60 people aboard in October 1928, and the following year the Graf Zeppelin made a number of successful intercontinental flights.

The Vickers R100 airship made its maiden flight in December 1929, but the disaster when the R101 crashed in France on its first flight to India, with the loss of 48 lives, spelled the end of Government's interest in airships. The R101 was nothing to do with the Vickers project, but it meant that once again Barnes Wallis was redundant, in so far as airship design was concerned

He was, however, enlisted as Chief Structural Designer in a team of four in Vickers Aviation. Two others in this team were Captain

Mutt Summers, who was for many years Chief Test Pilot, and R. J. Mitchell, the designer of the renowned Supermarine Spitfire. That was in January 1930. Some unconventional inventions were to flow from this team.

Barnes Wallis, using his extensive knowledge of lightweight structures, invented the geodetic principal of construction. At its simplest, a geodetic form is a system of wires or tubes which are spirally wound around an imaginary tube, in opposite directions. At the points where these tubes or wires cross they are anchored with fishplates. This offered several advantages over the traditional form of plates bolted, rivetted or welded into solid structures – the structure was lighter in weight, it was able to flex which was not possible with the rigid structure, and because it had inherent strength from these windings, fewer cross beams were needed and so more working space was created.

The first aircraft of note to use this geodetic design was the Wellesley – built to fly the long distances dreamed of by Wallis. It flew non-stop from Egypt to Australia, a total of 7,150 miles, in November 1938. A production line for this bomber was set up, but only 177 were built.

Meantime, Barnes Wallis was working on its successor, the Wellington – a twin-engined bomber, that made a substantial contribution to Bomber Command's early raids. It was also flown on long distance patrols over the Eastern Atlantic, later fitted with the Leigh Light. More than 11,000 Wellingtons were produced. A later variant was the Warwick, which, in Coastal Command service, was used for meteorolgical and air/sea rescue duties.

In 1942, Barnes Wallis, as Assistant Chief Designer, had been instructed to press on with the detailed development of a four-engined bomber, to be named Windsor. Handley Page were producing the Halifax, Avro the Lancaster and Short the Stirling, so Vickers had to be able to offer Government a bomber that had the edge on the others. The Windsor was to have an undercarriage under each engine nacelle, and to be fitted with remote controlled defensive armament, so enabling a heavier bombload by a reduction in crew weight. Only 3 Windsors were flown.

Vickers Armstrong's Aviation Department's main base was at Weybridge, in the famous Brooklands motor racing circuit. Within the small oval area of this circuit, assembly plants and an airfield had been constructed. As the activity expanded to meet wartime demand, the design department was re-located down the road at Burhill Golf Club house, and nearby was Silvermere Lake.

Barnes Wallis was no man to confine his inventiveness and probing mind to the design of airframes. He became interested in the shock wave effects of deep penetration explosives – what if one was able to create a massive explosion near the submerged base of an apparently impregnable structure? What kind of rupture would ensue? His designs included Grand Slam, a bomb of 22,000 lbs, and Tallboy of 12,000 lbs. 45% of the weight of Tallboy was Torpex explosive, and when dropped from 20,000 feet would penetrate 100 feet of earth, causing lethal shock waves.

He was aware that scientists had been quietly appraising target opportunities within Germany, in the event that the threatened war became a reality. One line that was being pursued was to deprive the heavy industries that were flourishing in the Ruhr valley, and the workforce, of the vital water supplies obtained from that river and its tributaries.

Over scores of years enquiring minds had been pondering how to develop the technique used in marine warfare during the early days of cannon, in which some of the cannon balls were made to ricochet off calm water, during close quarter engagements. Barnes Wallis would excogitate new applications while relaxing at his home in leafy Surrey.

It was not surprising that his ideas on how this ricochet property of a moving sphere could be put to practical use would find a readier ear within the Admiralty than within the Royal Air Force, and the Navy was still hampered in its all-out war against the U-boats by the lurking threat from the German capital ships. Perhaps he had found a way to put them out of action without having to chase these powerful ships across the high seas.

His first experiments in observing the flight characteristics of a sphere when propelled at a narrow angle over water were made in a rig-up in his garden. From those simple trials, he progressed to using a catapult to launch small balls across Silvermere Lake. Various surface shapes of the ball were used, including the dimpling that is used on golf balls. The key to making the balls bounce with some degree of predictability lay in the spin that was imparted at the time of the launch. Applying back spin to the ball extended the flight path, i.e. the distance between successive bounces and it reduced the exit angle below the angle of impact, i.e. the flight path moved nearer to being parallel to the water surface as the flight progressed.

The work of developing the spinning sphere was transferred to the Teddington water tank, which enabled flight paths and underwater travel to be closely monitored. There, Wallis was able to show that the sphere could be made to spin backwards, to bounce in a predictable fashion and along a designated path, then when it encountered a solid vertical surface, to work its way down the side of that surface, the contact being maintained by the spin. The principle had been proven.

It was late Spring of 1942 – when the war at sea was being dominated both by the U-boat packs and by the hit-and-run tactics of the German battle cruisers.

A demonstration was arranged at the Teddington testing tank for the benefit of Admiral Renouf and members of the Board of Admiralty. Barnes Wallis arranged for a wax model of a battleship to be moored, broadside on, several hundred feet up the tank from the launching gantry. He then fired 2 inch diameter balls at the ship. After hitting the freeboard, there was no tendency for it to bounce back; instead, the sinking velocity of the ball combined with the residual back spin caused the ball to move towards the ship. By adjusting the density of the ball, he was able to make a spinning ball pass right underneath the ship. A most impressive demonstration, which removed any doubt about the application of the principle.

Admiral Renouf was a strong supporter, and he persuaded the Board of Admiralty to appoint a representative (Lane) to attend later tests and to maintain an effective liaison.

The significance of the ability of the bouncing ball to be made to pass under the hull of the ship was not lost on this audience. They were all well aware that the 'soft underbelly' as Churchill called it, was the lowest part of the hull nearing the keel. If the ball could be made into a bomb, and that bomb be made to explode at a pre-set depth. . .

The size and detailed design of the prototype bomb had to depend on the type of aircraft from which it would be launched, and the method of launching. As the development of the 'bomb' was an extra-mural activity at Vickers Armstrong, it was natural that its Wellington bomber should be selected as the trials type. Design work could go ahead while discussions would take place within the Scientific Committee, of which Sir Henry Tizard was Chairman, as to which types of aircraft might be operationally the most suitable.

Wallis was, as might be expected, using what later came to be known as 'lateral thinking'. He realised there would be problems with wave heights greater than those used in the experiments. He wrote to Sir Henry indicating that a cylindrical shape may be preferable to that of a sphere, with that cylinder being lowered on a rope from beneath an aircraft flying at 50 feet. The rope, wound round the the axle of the cylinder, would act like the rope that used to be wound around the old-fashioned spinning top. The mind boggles today at the idea of using such a primitive device.

That method of spinning the weapon was quickly abandoned in favour of the more positive electrical and hydraulic options – but the important thing was that Barnes Wallis had succeeded in capturing the imagination of very senior service officers and scientific advisers in the potential of this new weapon. On 12th July 1942, the Deputy Director of Scientific Research (Armaments) Lockspeiser authorised a total of £2,000 to cover:–

   i. Water tank experiments with model bombs, including those already authorised and carried out,
  ii. Wind tunnel experiments with model bombs,
 iii. Full scale tests, including the modification of a Wellington Mk III aircraft and the preparation of inert bombs for air dropping trials.[1]

The Director of Scientific Research in a memo to Lockspeiser of 14th July 1942 talks of the case for restricting Wallis' spherical bomb to one of about 30″ diameter, with the comment: "It would be a pity if Wallis did his full scale work on something unnecessarily large". Lockspeiser replied the next day:–

"The original bomb was 45″ and could only be carried in Lancasters specially modified for the purpose. Because of this storage difficulty, a smaller bomb of 38″ is now in development. Wallis is proposing a 54″ bomb to conform with density and charge weight requirements against capital ships" Then, after referring to large bombs requiring specially modified aircraft as being uneconomic and that it was hopelessly impracticable to modify our bombers whenever a new type of bomb was proposed, he continued:–

[1] Public Record Office PRO AVIA 15 – 3933

"The only justification for departing from this principle seems to be in the case of special land targets, small in number, which it is very desirable to destroy and which might therefore justify the setting aside of special flights for the purpose. Dams are a case in point".[2]

At a meeting in Vickers House in London in August 1942, the Ministry of Aircraft Production, Admiralty, Air Ministry and Vickers Armstrong decided to start trials of the bomb on the Fleet Range near Portland, Dorset. This range is part of a stretch of fresh water, known as East and West Fleet, that is protected from the sea by a gravel ridge called Chesil Beach. Part of it is a swannery and thus a bird sanctuary.

The prototype had to be of a diameter that could be accommodated within the bomb bay of the trials Wellington – and the Admiralty placed orders with Oxley Engineering for practice spheres of 54 inch diameter.

The nature, positioning, weights and balancing of the components that would ultimately be installed in the sphere, and the nature of the surface skin, had to be evaluated individually and in combination. A ground test rig was set up to make the evaluations. Some of the matters that had to be resolved were: What type of detonating pistol would be used and where would it be positioned? How should the Torpex explosive be stored – and what proportion of the total weight could be assigned to the explosive charge? What materials should be used to represent the explosive in the inert versions? How strong must the outer casing be to withstand the force of impact during its progress over the water and when impacting against the target? Deformities in the skin on impact could cause the weapon to adopt erratic paths.

There was also another interesting question that had to be resolved very early on – in flying trials. Was there any, even remote, risk that one or more weapons of considerable bulk spinning at 1,000 rpm or so within the fuselage could have a gyroscopic affect on the stability of the aircraft? There was a fear that the gyroscopic effect of the bombload could make the aircraft difficult to control during the critical minutes of the attack

The Admiralty was keen to ensure that effort was not diverted away from the equally vital targets of German and perhaps Italian

[2] PRO AVIA 15 – 3933

capital ships at anchor. It is this potential use of the weapon on which we will now concentrate.

Bad weather on the range delayed the next flight testing until 15th December. That same Wellington had been flown to RAF Warmwell, a few miles inland from Weymouth, from where it made observed runs across the range. Two different spheres were used, one smooth surfaced and the other dimpled as on a golf ball. Mutt Summers was instructed to dive at full speed and to release the spheres at 60 feet height. Both spheres or "stores" broke up on impact; one was recovered after a long search by Barnes Wallis in a rowing boat, and he was pleased to note that it was buckled but had not broken up.

Further urgent experiments were made, with smooth and dimpled stores, strengthened by additional welding, and then by adding more ribs. Wooden stores with recording instruments installed were also dropped to gauge impact forces and other data.

Trials on 9th January 1943 from Warmwell achieved mixed results. A steel store broke up on impact with the water. The next suffered from a release mechanism malfunction, and it fell onto the land. That night, additional welding was carried out on a smooth sphere, which next day was dropped at 290 mph IAS at 100 feet and at 980 rpm. Although it, too, broke on impact, it was measured as having bounced to a height of 55 feet in a single bounce.

Back there again on 23rd January, Mutt Summers started the Fourth Trial by dropping a wooden sphere which bounced some 20 to 22 times. A simulated boom was set up across the range, and later that day, another wooden sphere was bounced over it. The mechanical and design problems were persisting, but the wooden spheres proved yet again that the principle was sound.

The team was back at Chesil Beach again on 5th February, this time achieving great success with smaller wooden spheres. They were 3 feet 10 inches in diameter and smooth surfaced. Dropped from heights of 145 down to 80 feet at a speed of 300 mph IAS, and revolving at 425 to 450 rpm, the spheres achieved a range of approximately 1,300 yards – a considerably greater distance than was predicted in the initial model experiments.

The introduction of the smaller diameter sphere was mostly as a result of the keenness of the Admiralty to have at the earliest date an operational version of this weapon or store.

The target capital ship to be chosen for the first operation would be at anchor. As the attack would have to be made in daylight it would have to be carried out by fast-moving aircraft. So the store to be used would have to be considerably smaller than that envisaged to be carried by the heavier aircraft planned for use in attacking the dams. This meant that while trials were continuing using the 54 inch diameter prototypes, the development work would have to move off into two different streams.

One of these, to be codenamed *Upkeep,* would culminate in attacks on the dams, using the larger diameter stores carried in Lancaster aircraft. The second, codenamed *Highball,* would involve Mosquito aircraft carrying the smaller stores in attacks against surface vessels. A third variation, codenamed *Baseball,* was an Admiralty dream, which involved mounting a large mortar in the bows of a motor torpedo boat (or gunboat), from which a small bouncing bomb would be fired against enemy ships. That last idea hung around for a couple of years before being consigned to the waste paper basket.

On 29th January 1943 Vickers Armstrong agreed to put in hand the manufacture of the smaller, 36 inches diameter, *Highball* stores at their Crayford works.

Inter-Service competition now began to surface. The Ministry of Aircraft Production (MAP) and the Admiralty, in these early days of 1943, had agreed to 'full priority' in the development of the smaller stores, *Highball,* to be carried by Mosquito aircraft against naval targets. Barnes Wallis was offering to have these aircraft available for operations within six to eight weeks – a brave, and almost reckless, commitment. He had a tremendous workload. Mosquito aircraft were in great demand for other RAF duties. The technical problems of the store were still being worked on. The Chief of Air Staff's assistants and advisers had not been persuaded that this *Highball* stream should overshadow the matter of the destruction of the dams.

It is interesting to note here that at an earlier stage in the war, the Board of Admiralty had agreed that the principle burden of carrying out long-range maritime reconnaissance, land-based air cover of convoys, and anti-shipping attacks along the Occupied coasts should fall on the Royal Air Force Coastal Command provided that Admiralty approval was obtained if other than maritime targets were contemplated. While the co-operation between Coastal Command and the Navy worked very well most of the time, this gave the Admiralty the right of say in matters such as the use of *Highball.* (It also created the strange anomaly within the RAF that other commands, such as 2nd Tactical Air Force, could attack ships, harbours and port installations, yet Coastal Command strike aircraft, Beaufighters and Mosquitos, were not permitted to attack airfields, railways etc.)

In many respects, February 1943 was a crisis month for Barnes Wallis and his projects. Air Vice Marshal Linnell, Chief of Research and Development at the MAP, was reluctant to sanction the development of what he called the *Big Highball* because that could divert the efforts of Barnes Wallis and the design team away from the Windsor B.3.42 four-engined bomber project. But on 10th February, Wallis learned that Linnell had ruled that nothing more should be done about the Lancaster project (*Upkeep*), but that work on the *Highball* project must continue.

Two days later, Linnell elaborated on his earlier statement, saying now that *Upkeep* must await the completion of the *Highball* tests. He added that an *Upkeep* attack should be carried out by a sufficient number of aircraft otherwise surprise would be lost.

The Commanders-in-Chief of Bomber and Coastal Commands had, of course, been kept informed of the developments. On 18th February 1943, Air Marshal Sir Arthur Harris, C-in-C Bomber Command, wrote to the Chief of Air Staff, Air Chief Marshal Sir Charles Portal:–

"With some slight practical knowledge and many previous bitter experiences on similar lines I am prepared to bet that the *Highball* is just about the maddest proposition as a weapon that we have yet come across and that is saying something." [He then talks about previous projects called *Toraplane* and its derivatives, and the *Johnny Walker*.] "With all those things we were pressed to start earmarking and modifying aircraft and training crews for months, and in some cases years, before the weapon had been developed to the stage where it became a convincing failure.

"The job of rotating some 1,200 lbs of material at 500 revs per minute on an aircraft is, in itself, fraught with difficulty. The slightest lack of balance would just tear the aircraft to pieces and in the packing of the explosive, let alone in rotating it packed in balance during rotation, are obvious technical difficulties. I am prepared to bet my shirt, a) that the weapon itself cannot be passed as a prototype for trial inside six months, b) that its ballistics will in no way resemble those claimed for it, and c) that it will be impossible to keep such a weapon in adequate balance either when rotating it prior to release or at all in storage, and d) that it will not work when we have got it.

Finally we have made attempt after attempt to pull successful low attacks with heavy bombers, they have been, almost without exception, costly failures. In these circumstances, while nobody would object to the *Highball* enthusiasts being given one aeroplane and told to go away and play while we get on with the war, I hope you will do your utmost to keep these mistaken enthusiasts within the bounds of reason and certainly to prevent them setting aside any number of our precious Lancasters for immediate modification".

Here was a man who did not believe in mincing his words, some of which were to prove prophetic. He mistakenly refers to *Highball* in place of *Upkeep*.

In his reply dated 19th February, Sir Charles Portal tried to tone down Harris' comments, saying that he had the greatest respect for Harris' opinion on all technical and operational matters and he agreed with him that it was quite possible that the *Highball* project may come to nothing [repeating the same error with the codename], but he did not feel inclined to refuse Air Staff interest in these weapons, "since the whole conception was far simpler than that of the two other projects which you mentioned.

We know that the full size mock-up of *Highball* does what is claimed for it unless the cinema lies."[3]

Dr. Barnes Wallis was asked to go to the High Wycombe headquarters of Bomber Command, where his reception by its chief was, to say the least, distinctly hostile. He must have been cheered though by the final, formal approval by MAP on 22nd February for the modifications to be made to two Mosquitos for *Highball* trials.

The very next day 23rd February he was told by his boss, Kilner, that the two of them were to go straight away from Weybridge to Vickers House in London to see the Chairman of Vickers Armstrong, Mr Craven. There, Wallis was told by his Chairman that he must drop further work on the larger bomb. Craven said that Wallis was 'making a thorough nuisance' of himself at the MAP, and by involving Vickers Armstrong directly or indirectly was damaging the firm's interests, and that, moreover, he had offended the Air Staff. Linnell had told Craven "to stop his [Wallis'] silly nonsense about the destruction of the dams". But the ban did not affect work on *Highball*.

The Chief of Air Staff, Sir Charles Portal, must have contacted AVM Linnell at MAP, who replied to Sir Charles asking if the operational use of the bomb had been considered at a high level. "We are now going ahead with the design and manufacture of a smaller type and at the same time we are converting Mosquitos to take this bomb. I presume that these will be used for attacks against ships." He goes on to talk about the loss of surprise if the smaller *Highball* was used before the attack on the dams. "It is quite obvious that it is a waste of time for us to rush on with the manufacture of the small bomb and the modifications of the Mosquitos if they are not to be used until the big bomb and the modified Lancasters are ready. It is very doubtful if these latter could be made ready 'till mid or late Summer."

On Friday 26th February, at a meeting attended by senior representatives of Air Minstry, MAP, and Vickers-Armstrong – including Craven, Wallis and Chadwick, the designer of the Lancaster, the need for utmost security was stressed, and Linnell announced that the Chief of Air Staffs wanted "every endeavour" to prepare aircraft and weapons for use in Spring 1943. The *Upkeep* project was back in favour again, and it was to have priority over the B.3.42 Windsor bomber project at Vickers Armstrong and over other projects at Avro. Three Lancasters should be prepared for trials as soon as possible with the full *Upkeep* apparatus. Eventually another 27 Lancasters would be similarly modified and 150 mines [stores] produced. The Air Ministry representative introduced for the first time to this group the date of 26th May as the last date for carrying out the operation against the dams in 1943, so all the aircraft and stores should be ready by 1st May.

Dr. Barnes Wallis must have been totally bewildered by these instructions and the counter-instructions that followed with machine-gun rapidity. He had been belittled by the chief of Bomber Command, given a rocket by his own chairman, and was still wrestling with the detailed design problems that kept eluding him. He was probably unaware at that time that Linnell had told the Chief of Air Staff that the *Upkeep* aircraft and stores could not be ready until mid or late summer and almost in the same breath was telling a meeting that all should be delivered by 1st May!!

Dr. Barnes Wallis had made a very substantial contribution to

Britain's aviation history, but the ending of the war allowed him to work with greater freedom, as the wartime committee structure through which much of the development had to be conducted was, in itself, tremendously demanding. As Head of Research he was still intrigued with the ideas of long distance travel by large groups of people and freight. He had visions of an aircraft that would be capable of flying at speeds of Mach 5 to 6, with sufficient fuel to fly around the world in under 4 hours – science fiction of the day, but how often is so-called science fiction brought to reality!

One idea, codenamed *Heyday*, involved a high speed underwater craft, travelling free from the uncomfortable wave movements that affected surface craft. This was abandoned when they hit the insurmountable problem of achieving a smooth aerodynamic flow along the entire length of the craft.

Supersonic travel was uppermost in the minds of aviation designers. Barnes Wallis worked on a variable sweep wing, shaped like a wild goose – the wings moved forward for low speed and back for high speed. Unmanned full scale trials of the *Wild Goose* were made from RAF Predannack, near the Lizard in Cornwall. Another variant was called *Swallow*. Vickers was also building at Weybridge the multi-role combat aircraft TSR2, which was cancelled as an economy measure by the Government when the aircraft was at an advanced stage.

Another interest was that of thermal insulation of aircraft structures.

Of course, he tried his hand in the field of guided missiles, including a design in which the wings and engine were stowed inside the tube for the launch stage. Another was a missile in which 90 grenades were stowed – to be spun out in groups of five as the weapon came to its targets. This could have been the genesis of the JP-233 bomb which was used in the Gulf War.

Sir Barnes Wallis died in 1979, aged 92 years.

A de Havilland Mosquito. (Mosquito Aircrew Association)

Bomb bay without doors to receive one Highball *store, showing aerody-namic sensors fitted during trials. (*Brooklands Museum*)*

Loading an inert Highball *store into the modified bomb bay of a Mosquito during trials from RAF Manston. (*Brooklands Museum*)*

An early version of an inert Highball *store used for spinning trials.*
(Brooklands Museum*)*

The major part of an early prototype bouncing bomb dropped from a
Wellington over the Fleet Range, Dorset, from where it was recovered in
1992. (author)

CHAPTER 3

The Creation of No 618 Squadron in Coastal Command

All the time that Barnes Wallis was preparing for the first trials of a prototype bouncing bomb, the Intelligence Services were at work to discover the German plans involving their capital ships. One source of reliable information was the British Naval Attaché in Stockholm, Capt. Henry Denham. (It was Denham who gave the first information in May 1941 that the *Bismarck* and *Prinz Eugen* had been sighted in the Kattegat en route to the Atlantic. The *Bismarck* was sunk during the engagement that followed.) So, in June 1942, Denham sent a coded signal to the Admiralty containing an accurate forecast of German naval plans for the Northern waters.

At that time, a large Arctic convoy, bound for Murmansk with war materials for the Russian offensive, was starting its perilous journey from Britain. The First Sea Lord, Admiral Pound, learned on July 4th by the Ultra Special Intelligence that the *Tirpitz* had put to sea. This appeared to confirm what had come through from Capt. Denham, and, despite receiving a further intelligence report that the German ship had not sailed, he decided that an attack on convoy PQ17 was imminent. Admiral Pound ordered the convoy to break up and scatter – a terrible mistake, as the merchant ships were then defenceless against the onslaught by the Luftwaffe and the Kriegsmarine that followed.

It was later reported that the Germans were planning to bring the *Tirpitz* back from Narvik Fjord to either Gdynia or Swinemunde for refit sometime late in 1942. Immediately, the naval and air operations planners started work on plans to attack her while she was on passage. The plan was codenamed *Operation Scrag*.[1]

The plan assumed that the battleship would be escorted by at least 6 destroyers. The convoy would stay within the 'leads', that is

[1] PRO AIR 20-1059

the deep-water channels between the mainland and the many islands of Norway, but they would be forced into the open sea at Startlandet, north of Bergen, because the leads are closed there by a rocky promontory. The convoy would get back into the leads until reaching Haugesund, from where the convoy would make a dash, at full speed, in the open sea into the Skaggerak and on to the Kattegat. The ship would therefore be exposed to attack for a large part of the voyage.

The convoy could probably make 15 knots through the leads, so could be expected to take 24 hours to reach Haugesund. Speeding up to a full 25 knots she would take 7 hours to get into the Skaggerak, and a further 24 hours would see her into port at Gdynia.

The first form of attack would be to mine the leads in the path of the convoy; it would then either have to make for the open sea or to anchor until the mines ahead were cleared. Next, she would be attacked by torpedo while she was exposed off Startlandet and again when south of Haugesund. There would also be concentrated high level bombing night attacks on the ship and nearby ports where she might seek shelter, as soon as these ports came within range of the convoy. The convoy would also be harrassed by daylight high level bombing.

The attcking aircraft would be provided by:–

Coastal Command – 2 torpedo, 2 general reconnaissance and 2 long range fighter squadrons, a total of 60 + aircraft;

Bomber Command – 65 Lancasters, 34 Wellingtons, and 22 Stirlings, to lay mines and carry out night bombing, 121 aircraft in all;

USAAF – would provide an unspecified number of Fortresses and Liberators for daylight high-level bombing.

The tragedy of Convoy PQ17 and now this massive assembly of aircraft gives some impression of the importance to the Allies of taking the *Tirpitz* out of the war.

On 16th November 1942, a further Intelligence report stated that the move of the convoy was imminent. But it did not take place and the *Operation Scrag* was stood down.

On 28th February 1943, an important paper was issued by the Air Staff headed "Appreciation on the Relative Priorities to be accorded to the Mosquito and Lancaster Spherical Bomb Projects".[2]

[2] PRO AIR 6-63

It warrants inclusion here in full:–

"Weapons:– The spherical bomb for the Mosquito, which will carry two, weighs 950 lbs. It has a charge weight of about 600 lbs, a diameter of 35 inches, and is launched at low level with a back spin of approximately 500 r.p.m. The range will be about three quarters of a mile. The weapon is intended primarily for:–

   i. the attack of the *Tirpitz* when protected by booms,
   ii. the attack of major naval units and other shipping at sea.

"The spherical bomb for the Lancaster will weigh about 11,000 lbs, with a charge of about 7,000 lbs and a diameter of 54 inches. Its general performance will be similar to that of the Mosquito weapon. Its purpose will be the destruction of the Möhne Dam, but other uses may be found for it subsequently. Instructions have been given for the development and production of these weapons and the requisite modification of the aircraft on the following scales:–
   i. 2 squadrons of Mosquitos and 250 bombs of 950 lbs each, and
   ii. 2 squadrons of Lancasters and 100 bombs (11,000 lbs).

Objectives:–
   i. The destruction of the Möhne Dam would be a catastrophe for the Germans. Large industrial areas would be flooded and water supplies would be denied to the Ruhr industries and the industrial population.
   ii. The sinking of, or serious damage to, the *Tirpitz* would greatly improve the naval situation by releasing certain major units for service in other theatres.

Tactical Considerations:–
"The Möhne Dam – no attack has yet been made on the Möhne dam and the enemy does not appear to have taken precautions which would preclude success. Reconnaissance, however, reveals the presence of an anti-torpedo boom across the dam. The enemy is thus alive to the possibility of torpedo attack. Tactically, on the information so far available regarding performance of the bomb, a night operation against the dam offers considerable prospect of success. Its success, however, is largely dependent on the water level. The water level will probably fall during the summer months, and it is estimated

at present that an attack is unlikely to be effective after the end of May. This estimate may need revision in the light of the rainfall experienced. If the Möhne attempt is to be made, the aircraft must be modified, the weapons produced and the squadrons trained in their use by the early part of May. Surprise is essential to success, as in view of the tactical limitations imposed by the weapon, it will be a simple matter for the enemy to dispose defences which would make the operation impractical.

ii. *Tirpitz* – the prospects of a successful attack against the *Tirpitz* in Trondheim are increased as a result of the superior performance of the Mosquito compared with current torpedo bomber types and of the characteristics of the bomb. These are such that the boom defences will be rendered ineffective and detonation will occur below the armoured belt of the ship. A night attack will not be possible owing to the difficulty of seeing the target even in moonlight against the dark background of the land and in the face of searchlights and gun defences, and in view of the navigational difficulties involved in a low level approach to the target from outside RDF (Radio Direction Finding) cover. We would therefore have to rely on a low level approach and attack in daylight. All precautions have clearly been taken to protect the *Tirpitz*, and the success of an attack, even with these new weapons, would be problemmatical, and, in any case, costly.

"Time factor:– Development and production of both projects is proceeding simultaneously. As far as can be determined at present there is no clash between the two programmes and neither could be accelerated appreciably at the expense of the other. The target date for the Lancaster project is 1st May. This may be possible of achievement but a firm estimate cannot be made until detailed investigations now in hand have been completed.

"The Mosquito programme may well be completed in May.

"Priority of Objective:– Weighing the chances of success of both operations, it is clear that they are much greater in the case of the Möhne Dam. An unsuccessful attack on the *Tirpitz* is almost certain to lead the enemy to reviewing his boom defence measures. This review would automatically embrace the defences of the Möhne Dam, and would prejudice the possibility of a successful attack. The reverse arguments apply in the event of the Möhne attack being launched first, but in this case as the attack will be made at night, and in the presence possibly of unpractised and denuded defence personnel, the behaviour of the weapon may not be observed.

"In addition to its use for the attack on the *Tirpitz*, the Mosquito weapon may have so great a value in anti-shipping attack as to justify its employment in this role at an early date, against the ships at sea. The weapon will be used tactically as a torpedo, generally at long range. In these conditions its characteristics may not be so easily determined or associated with its anti-boom possibilities. Nevertheless, it is considered that it should not be employed in this way until sufficient Mosquito squadrons have been equipped to ensure the maximum advantage from initial surprise and an adequate dividend before counter measures can be adopted.

"Conclusions:–
i. every effort should be made to launch the attack against the *Tirpitz* and on the Möhne Dam at the same time,
ii. if the Lancasters are ready in time for an attack on the dam in May they should be used whether or not Mosquitos are ready,
iii. if the Mosquitos are ready first they should not be used until it is known that the Lancasters cannot be ready by the end of May, if that should prove to be the critical date,
iv. the Mosquitos should be used first against the *Tirpitz* and this operation should not be undertaken until sufficient aircraft are available to take full advantage of surprise."

That paper brings out clearly the inter-relationship of the two operations. The critical date of 26th May as the last date on which the dams raid could be mounted stems from the fact that the winter rains would be continuing to fill the reservoir at a greater rate than the offtake of water from the reservoir until about May; the ideal water level for maximum effect of blast from *Upkeep* would be five feet from the brim; and the ideal phase of the moon for the attack would occur during the few days ending on 26th May.

This paper makes no reference to the opinion of the naval chiefs that, if the *Highball* was to be as effective as the scientists predicted, there should be simultaneous attacks on the *Tirpitz* and on Italian capital ships.

That very explicit paper was discussed on the last day of February, and it points up how much would have to be assembled for the two operations to take place not more than 85 days later.

Air Vice Marshal Norman Bottomley, Asst Chief of Air Staffs (Ops), wrote on 19th March 1943 to Sir Arthur Harris, C-in-C, Bomber Command, to tell him that the necessary steps were being taken to modify 20 Lancasters by 8th May – for an operation against the Möhne and, possibly, the Eder Dams. 40 inert bombs would start to be available, for crew training, by 30th March, and 60 HE (High Explosive) bombs would be ready by 30th April. Despite the earlier cynical comments by Sir Arthur Harris, the bouncing bomb weapon was to be used operationally by his Command.

Bottomley said that 30 Mosquitos were being modified, and would start to arrive from de Havillands/Vickers on 10th April, and by 8th May 16 of them should have been delivered. He writes:– "It is requested that a Lancaster and a Mosquito squadron be earmarked. It would appear that 139 Squadron is the only Mosquito squadron available."[3]

The official request to the C-in-C, Coastal Command, was dated 24th March saying:– "It is requested that a Mosquito unit be formed as soon as possible to undertake preparatory work for *Highball* operations. Bomber Command has agreed to provide an adequate number of trained crews and maintenance personnel to assist you in forming such a unit."

The choice of words and phrases in this second letter is rather strange. RAF personnel usually talk in terms of 'squadrons', rather than 'units', which could suggest that Bottomley had in mind something smaller than a typical squadron of two flights. But he says also that the unit should 'undertake preparatory work for *Highball* operations'. There were only 63 days remaining at the date of that letter until the last date for the Dams raid; that would leave precious little time to change from the 'preparatory' stage to the final run-in by the Mosquitos on their naval target.

Air Marshal Sir 'Jack' Slessor, at Coastal Command's Northwood

[3] PRO AIR 8-1234

Headquarters, received simultaneously a similar letter from the Under Secretary of State at Air Ministry. It advised that a meeting would be held the following day in Whitehall. The report that was presented to that meeting refers to the ports of Trondheim and Kiel as being within range of aircraft based in Britain.

Para 10 says: "Attacks against the other ports are beyond the normal operational range of Mosquito aircraft, and would involve the *acceptance of the possible loss of all aircraft*, that might be forced down in Swedish or Russian territory." (Author's italics.)

The *Tirpitz* was in lying in the shelter of Narvik Fjord, well to the north of Trondheim.

Sir Jack Slessor, who had only taken over from Sir Philip Joubert as chief of Coastal Command in February 1943, found himself charged with the duty of creating a new force of Mosquito aircraft which was to be fully operational by the middle of May – less than 50 days' time – with a weapon that was still in the development stage .

Coastal Command's only Mosquitos were in service with Photographic Reconnaissance Units and a Met squadron – in small numbers. Air Ministry had already indicated that the only likely source of aircraft for training, spares and crews with experience on the type was 139 Squadron, Bomber Command. But there was nothing to suggest that his counterpart, Sir Arthur Harris, was minded to release some of his most valuable crews – particularly as he had just committed Bomber Command to the rapid introduction of a Pathfinder Force to improve the effectiveness of his night bombings.

Sir Jack Slessor, and his Group commanders, had first to consider who should be selected to command this new Mosquito force – of at least one squadron strength. A very positive nomination by the AOC, 18 Group, Aubrey Ellwood, of Wing Commander G. H. Hutchinson, the Officer Commanding No. 235 Beaufighter Squadron, was readily approved. 235 Squadron had recently moved from RAF Chivenor, in Devon, to RAF Leuchars from where it operated at low level along the Norwegian coastline.

Wg Cdr Hutchinson, or "Hutch" as he was universally known,

was an experienced pilot from the first days of the war. He stood well over six feet, with the broad shoulders of a rugger player. His oval face framed a firm mouth above a pointed chin. In conversation he was quietly spoken, but when addressing a group, it became clear that he was a man who enjoyed authority. He was well respected by everyone on the squadron; he encouraged better performance from everyone, but was unhesitatingly firm with those who did not match up to the job, or thought that second-rate work would suffice. When in the formation behind Hutch, the crews knew that their leader was courageous but not foolhardy; an easy leader to follow. He was always a welcome addition to any group in the Officers or Sergeants Mess – and could out-drink most other mess members. He was an excellent choice, as it would take him only a few days to stamp his authority on this amalgam of crews.

Obviously the new squadron would have to borrow aircraft until the modified Mosquitos came off the production line. The only source was Bomber Command. But there were other considerations when it came to selecting crews, and the best fit appeared to be to combine the skills and know-how of trained Mosquito flyers of Bomber Command with the different skills of those who flew Beaufighters on shipping strikes.

Wg Cdr Hutchinson was given a copy of a Directive from the C-in-C, Coastal Command (CC/MS/7441/Trg) dated 27th March 1943 that Air Ministry had authorised the formation of a new squadron within Coastal Command, to be numbered 618, which would be formed on 1st April 1943 at RAF Skitten in the north of Scotland, and would be equipped with Mosquito aircraft. He had been selected to command this new squadron. Everything associated with this squadron was to be treated as TOP SECRET. The squadron was to be brought rapidly to a high level of operational capability within a few weeks – to undertake a daylight low level attack with a new weapon against the *Tirpitz*.

The immediate job to be tackled by Hutch was to find the aircrew to make up the squadron – at least 19 two-man crews in addition to himself and his observer. As this was to be a Coastal Command action, the normal healthy inter-Command rivalry suggested that the crews should come from the Coastal torpedo and fighter squadrons, such as No. 235 which he at present commanded. But no-one in those Coastal Command units had any experience of flying the Mossie, and there was insufficient time to convert a whole squadron onto the type. The crews that came from Coastal, and himself, would have to undergo a brief conversion course, in any case. The prime source of crews with Mossie experience had to be RAF Marham, in Bomber Command. Hutch was assured that there would be no problem in obtaining the release of selected personnel from their present squadrons; the commanders would be instructed to obey without question, and they would resolve the problems of filling the spaces in the squadrons.

The telephones at HQCC were buzzing as the detailed pieces of putting together the squadron were put into place. The Coastal Command crews would be sent to the Mosquito Conversion Unit at RAF Marham for concentrated training lasting not more than one week; during that time the crews from Bomber Command would prepare to move to Skitten, with the aircraft that were to fill the gap until the operational Marks were delivered.

Hutch chose from Coastal Command squadrons the men who were to be leaders of "A" and "B" Flights, both of whom had the charisma, experience and skills to lead in this dangerous mission. "A" Flight commander would be Flt Lt, acting Sqn Ldr C. F. (Charlie) Rose, DFC, DFM, while "B" Flight would be commanded by Sqn Ldr G. N. (Emjay) Melville-Jackson, DFC.

Charlie Rose was the exception in that he had experience on Mossies. Then a Flying Officer, he had flown DK289 from Bircham Newton on the first PAMPA met. flight on 2nd July 1942, and he flew the first operation – on 1st August – of the newly formed No 521 Met Squadron.

Included in the selection of crews were a number from 235 Squadron. Hutch flew back to Leuchars, and immediately told those aircrew who would be leaving with him (including the author) that they would be going the next day to take the Mosquito Conversion Course preparatory to joining a new squadron. Nothing more could be said about the future. The crews that had been flying on ops. that day were debriefed, told to go back and pack, given rail warrants then told that Hutch had ordered that there would be farewell parties that evening in the officers' and sergeants' messes.

Those were some parties! The normally staid civilian Mess Secretary in charge of the Officers Mess took his place at the improvised crease on the lounge cricket field, while others bowled mess china cups for him to swipe – fortunately, for only a minute or two. Then the officers who were leaving went with Hutch to the Sergeants Mess, where there were other high-jinks. The squadron was saying Cheerio to a much-loved man.

Some of us were lucky enough to be offered a ride the next day from Leuchars to Marham in the station Anson. Flt Lt 'Boosey' Pain flew the aircraft while the rest of us nursed our sore heads. The Officers Mess at Marham was, like that at Leuchars, a solid brick building, with accommodation adjoining and above the public rooms. 'Boosey' had intended to fly off but Hutch persuaded him to stay overnight. A few drinks at the bar before dinner and another party was under way. After dinner, in the lounge, we must have been a little noisy, as the Duty Officer respectfully asked us to quieten down – to no effect. Several other officers had a go at this, without success; then at about 23.00 hours a figure in a thick woollen dressing gown pushed his way into our circle, and commanded us to leave the mess there and now. Unfortunately for inter-Command relationships, one of our number laughed at the slightly balding, heavily moustached figure. We were pulled up with a jolt when he told us he was the Station Commander, Gp Capt Wallace Kyle, and was concerned that his aircrew were being prevented from getting the sleep that they so badly needed. We were told that the bar was out of bounds during our stay. In the sober light of day, it was a pretty fair punishment.

Next morning, 29th March – only 5 days after the Air Ministry letter to the C-in-C, Coastal Command – the former Beaufighter crews were taking their first look around the de Havilland Mosquito Mark IV. They were very impressed with what the instructors told them about its performance.

The Conversion Unit was unaware of the role of 618 Squadron, and not a lot could be said to them without arousing too much interest. So the individual crews took their turn along with those from Bomber Command – for a brief flight by the pilot with an instructor, then a couple of short familiarisation flights as a crew. Hutch called the crews together and told them that he considered that we were sufficiently competent to handle the aircraft and the rest of the familiarisation could wait until we were up at Skitten.

Meanwhile, on 3rd April, the first 53 other ranks arrived at RAF Skitten from Nos. 105 and 139 Squadrons, RAF Marham, and while they were unpacking that afternoon, they heard the familiar drone of the Rolls Royce engines as 8 Mossies from 105 and 139 Squadrons buzzed the airfield, lowered their undercarriages and came in – to a big welcome from their own ground crews.

Hutch was down at HQCC and Air Ministry attending the numerous briefings and discussions which were taking place at that time. He was to learn that at the same time that he had been selected to command this new squadron, Wing Commander Guy Gibson, a veteran Bomber Command pilot, was being briefed in his role as Officer Commanding a newly formed No 617 Squadron. That squadron was being equipped with a somewhat similar weapon, which was codenamed *Upkeep,* and they had a target date of *15th May.*

Gibson, when he first saw the models of his target dams, said his first feeling was; "Thank God, it's not the *Tirpitz*".[4]

4 "Enemy Coast Ahead" by Wg Cdr Guy Gibson, VC, DSO, DFC

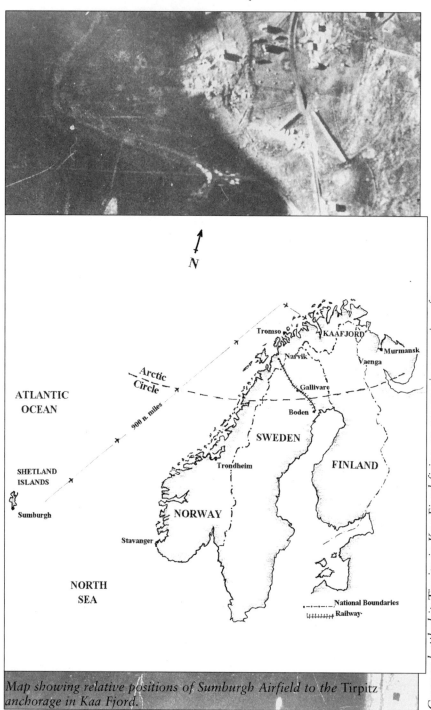

Map showing relative positions of Sumburgh Airfield to the Tirpitz anchorage in Kaa Fjord.

German battleship Tirpitz in Kaa Fjord firing on reconnaissance aircraft.

CHAPTER 4

The Squadron Shakes Down, and Wonders

Except perhaps for RAF Davidstow Moor, in the middle of Bodmin Moor, there cannot have been a more isolated spot on mainland Britain on which to build an airfield than Skitten. There is, in the far north east of Scotland, a triangle bounded on the long side by the Wick to Thurso road, and on the other two sides by the north and east coasts. Much of the area is wetland, including a sizeable lake, Loch Watten. The airfield was built to the north east of this loch, alongside a back road from Wick to Thurso.

The town of Wick was essentially a fishing port, whereas Thurso was the mainland embarkation port for sailors going to and from the major naval base at Scapa Flow, on the southern side of nearby Orkney. The railway line from Inverness made its way along the coast at Easter Ross, then turned inland to Lairg before returning to the north east coastline. At Helmsdale it turned inland again and, traversing the wetlands, it came to Georgemas Junction; the Wick passengers changed there for the short run past Loch Watten. The bulk of the traffic would be bound for Thurso. The wartime journey was scheduled to take just over 24 hours from London, but seldom was that possible.

There was a spasmodic bus service along the main 21 mile road from Wick to Thurso, so the men and women based at Skitten were mostly reliant on the 5 ton trucks that made frequent runs to Wick.

RAF Skitten was a satellite to the busy Coastal Command airfield of Wick, that bordered the town. Skitten was used as an overflow, and had been occupied variously by 86 (Beaufort), and 144 and 489 (Hampden) Squadrons. Two months before the arrival of 618 Squadron, the airfield had been used by a Special Commando Group which was flown to Norway to destroy the heavy water plant near Vermork, thus depriving Hitler of the chance to make the first atomic weapon.

The Station Commander, RAF Wick, Gp Capt Kyle, was also in charge of RAF Skitten. There was a small nucleus of RAF station staff, under the Station Admin. Officer, Sqn Ldr Tommy Thomson, and his WAAF Section Officer, Barbara Bulloch. They, and the newly appointed adjutant of 618 Squadron, Flg Off F. Hawley, did a great job in bringing together all the essential components of administration in a matter of days. The first signs of their efficiency were the Daily Routine Orders – DRO's – and daily flying programmes, which were on the notice boards the day after the first crews arrived from RAF Marham, 4th April.

Sqn Ldr Charlie Rose was at Skitten to welcome the first of the Bomber Command crews from Marham, and he wasted no time in getting the first navigation training flights under way the following day. The purpose of these two hour navigation flights was to quickly familiarise these crews with the geography of northern Scotland and Orkney and Shetland, as well as to begin to accustom them to flying for a long period at fairly low level over these northern waters.

The aircrew who were not on the flying detail were taken by truck to RAF Wick to spend time reading in the Operations Room. This, also, was to give them a picture of the operations of Coastal Command – by reading debriefings, and looking at photographs of the Norwegian coastline taken by reconnaissance Hudsons, or the Beaufort, Beaufighter or Hampden aircraft that were engaged in attacking enemy shipping.

Sadly, tragedy struck this new squadron very early on, when on the morning of 5th April, DZ 486 crashed into a hillside 10 miles SW of Durness, in Caithness, killing both the pilot, Flg Off Pavey and his navigator, Sgt B. W. Stimson. The funeral of Sgt Stimson took place on the afternoon of 10th April in Wick Churchyard; the bearer party was made up of Flt Sgts Halley and Thorburn, and Sgts Murray, Templeton, Walker and Mudd.

The weather on the 6th April, the day after that crash, was so bad – with wet fog on the moors – that three of the aircraft on navigation flights had to be diverted – to Dyce, Leuchars and Usworth near Sunderland.

The crews from the Mosquito Conversion Unit arrived by train on the morning of 7th April, so the nucleus of the squadron was in place. The crews had to get to know each other – and there was, of course, a lot of banter about Coastal Command crews having webbed-feet, and the Bomber boys only wanting to fly at night when they couldn't be seen. But each knew that the other was, also, hand picked and each respected the work that the other had been doing before being summoned to this squadron.

Two of the Bomber Command crews had participated in daring and spectacular raids on Berlin on 30th January 1943. On that day, both Göering and Göebbels were to make major speeches in Berlin, and one of them was probably going to claim that their capital city was immune from attacks by the enemy. Three Mosquitos of 105 Squadron, including Flg Off T. Wickham and Plt Off Makin, had bombed Berlin just at the time that Göering was about to speak.

That afternoon, 139 Squadron had taken their turn. Sgts. J Massey and R. C. Fletcher were in a flight of three Mossies that arrived over Berlin, in a clear sky, minutes before the second speech and they, too, let the Berliners know that their city was as vulnerable to bombing in daylight as any other target. Unfortunately, Sqn Ldr Darling, the leader, was shot down by flak after the attack. DFC's were awarded to Wickham and Makin, and DFM's to Massey and Fletcher.

In the middle of March, 16 aircraft from 105 and 139 Squadrons had raided Paderborn. Over the target Sgt Massey's Mossie DZ 477 had been hit by flak in the wing root, and with fuel leaking, he had had to cut the port engine. Once he had set off on the return he tried unsuccessfully to re-start the engine. Flying low as he approached the enemy coast, he was picked up by searchlights and again hit by flak. With his 'good' engine giving trouble, he had managed to nurse the aircraft back to Docking, where the Mossie was written off as it hit the windsock.

Another of the ex-Marham crews, Flt Lt Cussens and Sgt Munro had been forced to make a crash landing at Stradishall on 20th March, their hydraulics having been shot up during an attempted raid on marshalling yards at Malines.

During the week that the 235 Squadron crews were converting to Mossies, 105 and 139 Squadrons carried out low level bombing raids on targets such as the Phillips works at Eindhoven, Ehrang, Trier and Namur – during which one of 139 Squadron's aircraft was lost.

So it was not surprising that, now, these ex-Bomber Command crews were expressing their disappointment at being moved from these two Mosquito-experienced squadrons just at the time that Air

Vice Marshal Bennett had been given the authority to create the famous Pathfinder Group. That was to give a whole new dimension to the tactics of night bombing, and the crews really felt that they were missing out on that, while not having a clue what they were going to be doing as the alternative.

The Coastal Command crews explained what it was like to fly at very low level on reconnaissance along the Norwegian coast; then, if target shipping was located, what it was like to fly into the flak from the escort ships and the shore batteries, then probably to be attacked by FW190's from nearby airfields.

But none knew what the objectives of the squadron were. "Anyone know why we are here, and in such a hurry?" was the question on everyone's lips.

The mystery deepened with the arrival of a Flt Lt Hicks, a DAPM (an officer in the RAF Security Branch) with a posse of corporal service policemen. We were miles from anywhere – so why did we need all this security?

The answers started to become known with the return to the squadron of Hutch on 14th April. Meanwhile the crews had been allocated to flights:–

Allocation of Aircrew to Flights – April 1943

C.O. Wg Cdr G H B Hutchinson, DFC
Navigator: Flg Off F J French

"A" FLIGHT

Pilot	Navigator
Sqn Ldr CF Rose, DFC, DFM	Flt Sgt Jackson
Flt Lt DA Stephen	Flt Sgt JR Halley
Flg Off AS Cussens	Sgt AW Munro
Flg Off EH Jeffreys, DFC	Flt Sgt DA Burden 968
Flg Off GW Rennie RCAF	Flg Off W Embrey RCAF
Flg Off AT Wickham, DFC	Flg Off WE Makin, DFC
Plt Off LT Weston RNZAF	Sgt GR Brown
Sgt J Massey, DFM	Sgt RC Fletcher, DFM
Sgt J Walker	Sgt L Murray

"B" FLIGHT

Sqn Ldr GM Melville-Jackson, DFC	Flt Sgt A Umbers
Flg Off FS Foss	Flg Off J Groome
Flg Off K Hamlett	Sgt A Mudd
Flg Off HB McCready	Sgt F Templeton
Flg Off DJ Turner	Flg Off D Curtis
Plt Off AL Bonnett RCAF	Flt Sgt DR Burden 458
Flg Off HC Hopwood	Flt Sgt GG Thorburn
Flt Sgt AH Hilliard	Sgt JB Hoyle
Sgt K Ellis	Sgt RW Donald
Flt Sgt BC Roberts	Sgt FG Winsor

Adjutant & Administration:	Flg Off F Hawley
Engineer Officer:	Flg Off OR Marshall
Signals Officer:	Plt Off JE Murrells
Electrical:	Flt Sgt Matthews
	Sgt Thompson
Instruments:	Sgt Lucking
Stores:	Flt Sgt McArthur
Other NCO's	Flt S Cotton
	Flt Sgt Tansley
	Sgt Morrison
	Sgt W Petter

Sgt Jock Morrison was the 'old man' or father figure of the squadron, probably in his fifties. He somehow contrived to stay with the squadron when it went overseas.

Crews from Coastal Command were:
    No. 235 (Beaufighter) Squadron:–
        Wg Cdr Hutchinson DFC & Flg Off French.
        Flg Off Foss and Flg Off Groome
        Flg Off Hamlett and Sgt Mudd
        Flg Off Turner and Flg Off Curtis
        Flt Sgt Hilliard and Sgt Hoyle

    No. 143 (Beaufighter) Squadron:–
        Flg Off Jeffreys DFC and Flt Sgt DA Burden 968

    No. 236 (Beaufighter) Squadron:–
        Plt Off Bonnett and Flt Sgt DR Burden 458

    No. 248 (Beaufighter) Squadron:–
        Sqn Ldr Melville-Jackson, DFC and Flt Sgt Umbers
        Flt Sgt Roberts and Sgt Winsor

    No. 521 Met. Squadron:–:
        Sqn Ldr Rose DFC DFM and Flt Sgt Jackson

Crews from Bomber Command were:
    No. 105 Squadron:–
        Flt Lt Stephen and Flt Sgt Halley
        Flg Off Wickham, DFC and Flt Off Makin, DFC
        Flg Off Hopwood and Flt Sgt Thorburn
        Flg Off Cussens and Sgt Munro
        Sgt Walker and Sgt Murray
        Flg Off DL Pavey and Sgt Stimson, who sadly were killed on
           5.4.93. (Replaced in "B" Flight by Flt Sgt Roberts and Sgt
           Winsor.)

    No. 139 Squadron:–
        Flg Off Rennie and Flg Off Embrey
        Plt Off Weston and Sgt Brown
        Flg Off Macready and Sgt Templeton
        Sgt Massey, DFM and Sgt Fletcher, DFM
        Sgt Ellis and Sgt Donald

Charlie Rose and his navigator, Flt Sgt Jackson, flew off to Manston on 7th April, and, as Hutch was still in conference, Sqn Ldr 'Emjay' Melville-Jackson was acting C.O.

The airfield was typical of the wartime layout – with good tarmac runways, dispersed flight huts, and the domestic quarters adjoining the operations block, between the flying control building and the road. Strangely enough, the gymnasium was located about half a mile along the road to Wick – yet there appeared to be plenty of space within the airfield perimeter. The ops. block, a single storey building of breeze block, and painted camouflage green like other buildings, was the scene of some activity by the carpenters and other trades. The windows were blocked in with black painted plywood, on the inside of which were also blackout screens. The doors were changed for stronger ones, and heavy locks fitted on each door.

In those first few days there was little to do when off-duty other than to enjoy a drink in the bar or, if fine, to walk across the heather to the loch or to Sinclair Bay. The first persons to reconnoitre Wick came back with the alarming news that it was a dry town – that meant that it did not boast a pub or bar. Who selected this God-forsaken place for us to do whatever it is we have been brought here for? Flt Lt 'Hicky' Hicks, the DAPM, put his police-trained mind to work, and came back from Wick with the news that Mackays Hotel would be able to provide alcoholic drinks provided that they were ordered at the same time as a dinner. This did not give the diner the right to order a drink in the dining room. Hicky explained the system – the driver of the morning truck into Wick would go to Mackays and order so many dinners for that evening. We would arrive very early evening, and would be shown into a lounge where the drinks would be served, and into which we would be locked until dinner was served. That ensured that we would not be conspiring to let the locals in to drink with us. We were finding out lots of things, but had yet to know the reason for our being there.

Immediately that Hutch rejoined his squadron, he called a meeting of all aircrew in the ops. room. As they queued to get into the ops. room itself, the security police checked each name against a clip-board list. Inside, the aircrew were joined by Hawley, the adjutant, and Hicky the DAPM.

The room fell silent as Hutch rose to his feet, on the small platform at the end of the room. What was he about to reveal?

"Gentlemen, I'm sorry that I wasn't here to welcome you when you arrived, but I was called to Coastal Headquarters for an update briefing, and, of course, a few meetings.

"You've all been wondering what you are doing here and, probably, why no-one has said anything about that since you arrived. Well, I am now going to set it all out in front of you, so we'll all know, from here on, what we are going to be doing.

"Before I go any further, I must tell you that each of you has been specially selected to join this squadron, and that the particular operation for which we are now training is going to be dangerous, with possibly heavy losses. So, if any of you feel that you would not want to be part of this, you are free to say so now. So, if you want to opt out, please step forward. I promise you that you will be returned to the squadron from which you came, without any stain on your records whatsoever."

He paused – and must have been acutely aware of the momentary panic that had gripped each man present. Every man tried to keep stock still, lest his movements or even his expression, suggested that he was about to step forward. 'If I step forward, will I be the only one – or will there be a bit of a stampede?' That instant of doubt over – with no takers to the get-out offer – Hutch went on:

"Thank you, gentlemen, we are now all committed to the task. That task is to make a daylight attack on the battleship *Tirpitz* while it is at anchorage in one of the fjords up in the north of Norway. We will be using specially made Mossies to carry a new form of weapon which is in the final stages of development. Listen carefully, now – the target date for this operation is 15th May. That's about a month's time. So we've got our work cut out to get to the peak of our efficiency in that month.

"You are all aware of the service police at Skitten, and most of you know Flt Lt Hicks, the DAPM. Hicks and his men are here to enforce a total security blackout – and he will be telling you more of that in a moment. But before we move off security, let me make it clear that everything about this squadron is Top Secret. The success of the operation and our lives depend on Top Secrecy being maintained. No one outside this room must know anything about our plans – not the ground crews, not the station personnel, not your wife – no one. I will have no hesitation in ordering the court martial of anyone who breaks that rule. Don't let your tongue loose after a few beers in the mess – those could be your last beers for years. Do I make myself clear?

"The Mossies that we will be flying are in the production line right now, and will be flown in as available, starting in the next few days. So the Mossies that came from Marham for our training will be returned where they are badly needed as soon as we can do without them. The modified aircraft will be the bomber versions, too, with the perspex nose cone.

"The new weapon is a spherical bomb, which can be made to bounce across the water by using back-spin, and then when it hits the ship, it will continue spinning down the side of the ship until it is exploded on the underside of the ship by a preset fuse. The advantage of the bouncing is that the bomb can then get over the torpedo nets which are always strung around the ship when it is at anchorage. We will be going into minute detail in the briefing that will take place every day.

"The raid has to take place in daylight, for reasons that are obvious to us. There are some problems that we have to work on, one being that right now the *Tirpitz* is, we believe, in a fjord which is just beyond the range of the Mossie – so a lot of people are working on schemes that will get us back from the raid.

"Outside of work there is not much to do up here, but each of you has to use spare time to make sure you are fit. We have a full-time squadron doc. and a dentist – so don't let us have toothache on the last day. There's a sports field and a gymnasium which we are going to make use of.

"You've got lots of questions, which we'll tackle as we go. But remember, those discussions take place here – no where else. That's a convenient point to hand over to Flt Lt Hicks."

Hutch leaving the platform was the signal for the men to relax, clear their throats and make the first whispered comments to their new pals. "No wonder they kept quiet about this. I'd have jumped off the train if I'd known!" "Maybe it's just as well this is all going to be over very quickly, 'cos we won't have to do this twice" etc.

Hicky took the floor. He was a former Metropolitan Police officer, who had been transferred to the RAF early on in the war. He was a very likeable person, and soon became a close friend of the aircrew.

His was a difficult job – but at least he would be staying on the ground.

"Gentlemen, you have heard the CO telling us that this is a Top Secret unit, and I want to elaborate on that by spelling out some of the rules.

"Firstly, I must remind you that you are all subject to the Official Secrets Act, which applies to all service personnel, and you remain subject to that Act until you are told otherwise. You cannot make up your own mind on when you might be free from its obligations.

"This operation has been classified Top Secret by the Chiefs of Staff of the War Cabinet. That shows you how important your operation is considered to be. Top Secret means that whatever information is imparted to you or comes to your knowledge can only be imparted to others by you to the extent that that other person has a need to know. In other words, you may make information available only to the extent that the other person needs it to get their part of the job done.

"A few examples will help to drive home the point. You have no need to tell one of your ground crew what the target is for him to do work on the aircraft. You must not assume that the person you are with knows all about it, unless he is one of the people here today or is a visiting senior officer who the C.O. will introduce.

"The trickiest part has to be what you may not tell your loved ones, or the girl friend, or the friendly bod in the bar.

"Over the next two days, each of you will be issued with a special security pass, which must not leave your possession. The flights will be curtained off by my corporals, and they will have been instructed not to let anyone through unless they show that pass. Don't think you needn't show it because the corporal knows you well enough. He'll turn you back until you show your pass.

"On your old squadron, the censorship of letters was probably done by duty officers. Here, letters written by anyone on the squadron will be censored by my Security staff. You are to post all your outgoing mail in the station post box – you are not to use post boxes out of camp, or even at RAF Wick. Now, a few words about what not to refer to in your letters – obviously, write nothing about the squadron, its number or the work it is doing, the type of aircraft and any of the flights that are being made, the number of personnel and personnel movements, this location and the weather conditions here. In your letters don't use initials or single letters in place of words, and – fond though you may be of your wife or sweetheart – xxx's are also banned. Reminders of these rules will be published frequently in SROs and in Squadron Daily Orders.

"Any questions then on Security?"

"Yes" said a voice from the back of the room, "Are you going to issue postcards – 'cos you've left us with damn all to write about?" A nice way of relieving the tension that Hicky had been building.

Hutch ended the meeting by announcing that tomorrow, 15th April, the AOC 18 Group, Air Vice Marshal Aubrey Ellwood, DSC, would be visiting Skitten from his Headquarters at Pitreavie, on the Firth of Forth.

At the close of that first meeting, the aircrew stood around in groups – making no move to leave the security of the Ops Room. The message that that was where they could talk freely had got through.

In the buzz, odd sentences came through: "God, they haven't given us much time to learn to fly these Mossies, let alone get to know what this bomb's all about."

"What do you make of the idea that the *Tirpitz* is outside our range, but we are still going to attack it?"

"The time to start worrying is when we're all sent to the swimming baths for swimming lessons!"

Aubrey Ellwood, (knighted in 1949, and living 'till the age of 95) was introduced by Hutch the next morning. He sought to put everyone at ease as he sat on the corner of the table to talk. He reiterated that the aircrew in 618 Squadron had been hand-picked from both Bomber and Coastal Commands so that, between them, they had the right mix of knowledge. The planning for the attack was going on at various levels from the Chiefs of Staff of the War Cabinet down. Winston Churchill was taking a personal interest in the development of the bouncing bomb.

We would be given every possible assistance from the technical people and the boffins, so we could expect to have lots of people visiting the squadron.

He had been told by the MAP that the first of the modified Mosquitos had nearly completed its trials and would be flying in to Skitten in two days time, 17th April. The RAF Photographic

Interpretation Unit were busy making models of the target areas, and these will be rushed up as soon as they had been cleared.

The following week, Gp Capt Tuttle, the SASO (Senior Air Staff Officer), 18 Group, paid a flying visit, mainly to satify himself that all was in order for the visit on 23rd April by the Inspector General of the RAF, Air Chief Marshal Sir Edgar Ludlow-Hewitt. Sir Edgar was taken to visit the newly arrived modified Mosquito, then gave a short address to the aircrew in the Operations Room. He also stressed the importance of finally putting the *Tirpitz* out of action, which previous missions had failed to achieve. He wished us great success in this undertaking.

For sure, 618 Squadron was not being neglected by the higher-ups. A near neighbour, living in Thurso Castle, was the Secretary of State for Air, Sir Archibald Sinclair. He paid several informal visits, staying for a drink in the mess, whenever his official duties allowed him to escape for a few days. He extended an open invitation for us to visit his family home when we wished.

The Coastal Command crews were getting used to flying the Mosquito – they all had a lot of time for the reliability and performance of the Beaufighter – but this Wooden Wonder was a truly great performer.

The aircraft had a wingspan of 54 feet and was over 40 feet in length. The Mark IV B. Bomber version had an all-up weight of around 21,000 lbs. At that time, it was powered by two Merlin 21 engines.

Entry for the pilot and navigator was through a small hatch on the starboard side, just forward of and slightly below the main spar. That entry hatch was also the escape hatch, should the crew have to bale out. The door was uncomfortably close to the starboard propeller, giving rise to the suggestion in Pilot's Notes that the starboard engine should be feathered before beginning the bale-out procedure.

The pilot had to enter first, and he was seated on his parachute pack. The navigator then climbed the telescopic ladder, carrying his large green navigation bag, hand-held camera and parachute pack. These two crewmen were seated side by side, with the navigator slightly set back. He was in fact sitting on the main spar, but positioned to give him access to the low-height space behind the pilot's seat.

The bomber version had a perspex nose into which the navigator could crawl when using the bomb sight for drift measurement and during bombing runs. The navigator would be wearing a thick white pullover under a battle dress jacket, on top of which his Mae West life jacket would be taped. To add to his bulk he wore his parachute harness, buckled in the area of his navel and with two clips at chest height onto which he would bang his 'chute pack if baling out became necessary. Fleece lined flying boots covered his lower extremity, and at the other end, he would be wearing his leather helmet, with a cable from his earphones to the plug-jack. This bulk meant that, when he crouched down and pushed his upper half through the small opening to the perspex nose, he had to be careful that nothing caught on the switches on the starboard side of the cockpit.

The wireless transmitter/receiver TR 1154/1155 was fitted in the very limited space above the main spar and under the streamlined canopy. To operate the set and get to the morse key, the navigator had to half turn in a crouched position.

The pilot started up the port engine first – a little throttle, constant-speed propellor controls fully forward, ignition on – then pressing the pair of starter and booster-coil buttons. The engine fitter would be operating the priming pump; then, usually with a few bangs as the excessive fuel burnt off, the engine fired. Pilots didn't like to leave the engines idling as the Merlins had a habit of overheating. But before taxying out, check bomb doors closed and selector in neutral, bomb control panel – all switches off and the guard closed, undercarriage emergency knob in normal and safety catch engaged. Taxying was straightforward with a good view over the nose.

Out at the take-off point beside the caravan, the pilot would run up each engine to 3,000 rpm to clear the spark plugs, check elevators, ailerons neutral, trim – a bit nose heavy – pitch fully forward, fuel checked and cocked to outer tanks, maybe 10° or 15° of flap, rudder slightly right, and rad. flaps open.

The green light given, the pilot opened the throttle fairly gently, port throttle slightly ahead of the starboard to counteract the tendency to swing to port. Brakes off and the aircraft almost leapt forward. As the speed built up, the tail was raised and at around 125 mph (108 knots) the aircraft unstuck. The pilot kept the aircraft level, raising the undercarriage quickly, to let the speed build up to 200 mph (175 knots), the safety threshold in the event that an engine cuts. Then into a climb, raising flaps and easing the throttles back to 170 mph (just below 150 knots), till achieving cruising height and speed.

Every pilot found that it was a great aircraft to fly, in spite of the fact that he lacked lateral vision because the engine nacelles protruded very close to the fuselage, and to starboard, the navigator partially blocked the view. Squadron aircraft were limited in the extent of aerobatics that pilots were permitted to perform, but looping and rolling off the top were quite safe manouevres, provided that the entry speeds were high enough. There was little tendency to stall, stalling speed being at around 113 knots.

Landing the bomber version called for a flatter approach than with the Mk VI fighter. Airspeed on the downwind leg was reduced to about 180 mph (156 knots), brake pressure checked, radiator flaps open and undercarrriage lowered; the most full fuel tanks selected, particularly after a long flight; propellor pitch control fully forward. Then flaps fully down, with a lot of nose-down trim, and the speed would be down to 160 mph (140 knots). Speed would be still falling off as the aircraft turned onto finals, the throttle being used to control the rate of descent. Crossing the threshold at about 15 feet, the speed would be 120 mph (105 knots). With throttles closed and the control column eased back the Mosquito would stall at 105 mph (90 knots).

A faulty engine was shut down by cutting the throttle, switching off the magnetos and pressing the feathering button. The propellor stopped with minimum drag. The aircraft was stable on one engine, with trim adjusted – but, of course, it was unwise to pull the aircraft into tight turns towards the dead engine. Landing with one engine feathered called for a long fairly steep approach, keeping the speed up above 160 mph (140 knots).

Normal cruising speed was 240 mph (210 knots) at low level, at heights up to about 5,000 feet.

Navigation exercises were usually flown at heights of about 2,000 to 5,000 feet. The routes of the outward and inbound legs had to be precisely plotted, to avoid the risk of coming too close to Scapa Flow and the potential fire power of the Royal Navy. A typical flight plan would include a first leg heading west-north-west to Rona, near to Skye, then north to the Faroes, and returning via the Shetlands. The objective was to hone the accuracy of navigation out of sight of land. While these were training flights, the navigator had to use every spare minute, with the pilot, in scanning the grey seas beneath, as that area was crossed by U-boats making their way to and from bases in Norway and in Germany.

On 16th April, DZ468 crash-landed at RAF North Coates. The crew, Flt Lt Stephen and Flt Sgt Halley were uninjured but the aircraft suffered Cat. B damage. The number of training aircraft had reduced to 6, with the operation planned for 29 days' time.

There was, of course, great excitement when the first of the specially modified Mosquitos – DZ531/G – was flown in from Weybridge on 17th April. The noticeable difference from the aircraft on which the training was being carried out was the absence of bomb doors – simply an open space with some slight fairings on the edges of the fuselage to maintain the clean lines of the fuselage. Within this hole, on either side were the cradles and spinning gear for the two bombs or " stores" that would be carried. The diameter of the stores was greater than the depth of the bomb bay, so the stores protruded as inverted humps below the fuselage. Hutch told us that a similarly modified Mosquito – DZ290/G – had been undergoing tests at the A & AEE, RAF Boscombe Down. The test pilot had flown it with and without dummy stores being carried. It was dived at full throttle at 390 mph ASI, when the pilot had to use maximum force to hold the aircraft in the dive. The force was only slightly less when the aircraft was dived without the stores. Boscombe Down gave full approval for the use of this modified aircraft at an all-up weight of 21,000 lbs.

On 19th April, to everyone's surprise, four Beaufighter Mk II, stripped down night fighters, appeared in the circuit. They were being flown by Air Transport Auxiliary (ATA) pilots, and had been made available for "training purposes" – somebody had really used their imagination! They were put to use as an airborne taxi service, even though they were uncomfortable for the passengers, who had to sit on the main spar beam or on the floor, and hang onto the airframe.

Charlie Rose flew in from Weybridge on 22nd April with the second *Highball* aircraft – DZ530/G. At the regular meeting in the Ops Room, Charlie gave long accounts of the trials that they had been taking part in, operating from RAF Manston. They had been working with Capt Mutt Summers and Sqn Ldr Shorty Longbottom of Vickers and some pilots from Bomber Command. Neither of them, nor, for that matter, Hutch, made any reference to No. 617 Squadron having been formed, or that its commanding officer, Wg Cdr Guy Gibson, was present at these trials.

The trials had taken place at a range at Reculver, along the mud flats on the south bank of the Thames estuary. Charlie reported that the wooden outer casings of the stores loaded with inert materials had broken up on first impact. Because of what was learnt at those trials, Dr. Barnes Wallis and his team made the decision on 18th April to remove the outer casing from the *Upkeep* store, leaving its final shape – as used in the dams raid – as a cylinder. The smaller *Highball* stores would all be encased in steel.

At the time of that report, the crews at Skitten had not seen either a prototype or any of the inert bombs, which they were told were being manufactured as a top priority, but they were well aware that time was slipping away without any 'final' practice flying. The fact that the 2 stores dropped from a Mosquito and 1 from a Wellington during the trials on 13th April all broke up on impact did not inspire confidence. There were signs of progress when Charlie returned from further trials on 30th April, during which 2 stores, with an outer steel casing, and filled to a positive buoyancy achieved a range run of 1,000 yards.

On 19th April, other trials were made at Ashley Walk against the armoured wall testing ground. A store with a new metal case and with aerated resin filling withstood the impact. Other trials at Angle, in South Wales, showed that the end plates of the stores had to be thickened to prevent buckling and that 5/8th" bolts were needed.

The people in the factories that were producing the casings must have been tearing their hair out at the constant changes that were being made in the design, while they were being asked to produce quantities of stores almost overnight.

A submarine depot ship, the *Bonaventure,* anchored in Loch a'Chairn Bhain, on the west coast of Scotland not far from Cape Wrath, was made available as a target ship on which to practise high-speed low-level runs in the confined space of a loch or fjord. Flying in vic formations, the Mossies would pass seawards of Cape Wrath, then climb quickly southwards before diving at full speed over the mountain on the north side of the loch. They would pull out of the dive and level off at 60 feet to stream across the calm water towards the ship, which was moored as close to the southern hillside as possible. At the very last moment, the leader and his wingmen would pull up, over the superstructure and wireless aerials of the *Bonaventure*, coming down again to hug the hillside as close as possible. In that way the gunners on the target ship and adjoining flak platforms would have the greatest difficulty in getting a clear shoot.

This was a highly dangerous exercise, with no room for manouevre, particularly on the escape climb over the heather and gorse bushes. As the speed fell off in the climb, the pilot had to guard against the tendency to 'sink' a few feet. Both the crew had to watch out for trees, possible cables and wires and the position of nearby aircraft, and, for the pilot, to watch his instruments intently. Shortly after this particular training exercise began, one of the aircraft was lost on the hillside as a result of that very thing. The work had to go on – but this was an easy simulation of what the real thing was going to be like. Here, the crews had made only a short flight from Skitten, and so were fresh and with eyes that hadn't tired from hours of strain while looking at grey seas. In the real situation, they would be tired from the long haul, highly charged with nervous energy, and with grim prospects of making some form of safe return back to Blighty.

More of the modified Mosquito Mk VI B's were arriving during the month of April, meaning that the number of hours flying could be pushed up. With less than a full complement of 20 aircraft, modified or otherwise, the squadron in April logged up 203 hours of low-level long distance navigation, 103 hours of low-level attacks on the target ship, and 23 hours of local flying – air testing, etc. Those figures did not include the flying that Sqn Ldr Charlie Rose was doing over the range at Reculver, where in the 16 days from 13th April, he dropped a total of 23 stores.

A tall, lanky ginger-haired man, Jim Rogerson, joined the squadron at Skitten as the resident representative of Vickers. He had worked with Dr. Barnes Wallis in the development of the bouncing bombs, so he was our expert. He was also a very accomplished jazz clarinet player, but had very little chance to perform in public in that isolated area.

Flg Off F. J. Rose was posted in as Armaments Officer, he having joined Charlie Rose for the trials at Reculver, flying from Manston.

Plt Off R. A. Payne arrived as Signals Officer early in May, and later that month, Plt Off L. O. Smith arrived as Engineer Officer.

Under guard, RAF trucks had brought in numerous wooden packing cases, which were placed in safe storage in the hangar, unopened and covered in tarpaulins. The ground crews had, of course, seen the gaping hole on the underside of the modified Mossies, so it did not need much imagination to work out that the contents of those boxes would finish up in the bomb bays.

Then, one day, the technical officers, NCO's and the armourers went out with one of the cases on the bomb trolley to the dispersals, where a crowd of excited aircrew stood waiting to see 'their' bomb. As the sides of the case were prised away, they were looking at a large steel ball, about 36 inches in diameter; closer inspection showed it to be what the navigators had learned at Nav. School was an oblate spheroid. That simply means that, like the Earth, it is a sphere but with the poles flattened, and protruding from the flattened sides were the spindle axles on which it would later be spun.

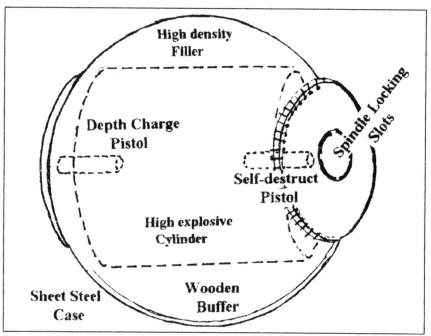

Schematc drawing of Highball weapon – no scale

The 'store' was eased under the belly of the aircraft, then Jim Rogerson and one of the armourers climbed alongside it so that they could winch it up, using the hand-wound winch fitted in the bomb bay. The axles were dropped into their driving shafts and locked into position.

"Give it a whirl!" said one of the onlookers, and the sergeant armourer did make it revolve slowly. "This is going to take some time to balance it properly before we dare switch on the drive motor," said the armourer – meaning that they didn't want an audience the very first time they had to rig up the installation. After a while the crowd dispersed.

Having the inert practise bombs gave the aircrews another task. Each of the aircraft had to have its magnetic compass swung twice at least – in those days satellite navigation sysytems had not even appeared in the sci-fi magazines – so it was vital that the P11 magenetic compass was precisely calibrated. The aircraft was taken to a remote corner of the airfield – as far as possible from interference from wireless signals or other magnetic fields. Then, with the instruments NCO aboard, the navigator would call for the aircraft to be pushed around in a circle, stopping at successive cardinal points of the compass. He would be using a hand-held bearing compass to take a magnetic bearing on the heading of the aircraft. This would be noted and relayed to the instrument NCO in the pilot's seat, who would read the bearing on the compass in the cockpit. The aircraft would be headed north, east, south and west, then north-east, south-east, south-west and north-west. The difference between the two sets of readings would then be plotted on a Compass Error card which lived next to the compass, allowing the pilot to adjust the course given by the navigator to the corrected course for that particular compass.

But, because on the outward flight the bomb bay would have in it a large amount of steel, which would not be there on the way back, the compass had to be swung, first with the stores loaded, then without the stores.

The accuracy of these variations from the correct magnetic headings was also being checked by the simple expedient of flying along the centre of each runway in both directions, then comparing the known runway headings with the readings of the aircraft compass.

Some navigation exercises were extended to become endurance tests, with two inert bombs loaded. Safety factors precluded flying these precious few aircraft and crew over the sea until the fuel gauges were showing zero, so a safety factor of about 30 minutes of straight and level cruising was built in. The consumption figures that were derived from these calculations were then telexed to Coastal Command Headquarters for comparison with the results that were achieved by Ministry of Aircraft Production scientifically measured tests, with a good correlation. Bomber Command had intimated that the normal range of a Mosquito Mk IVB was 1,200 nautical miles. Our exercises, combined with work done by Coastal Command, indicated that without any additional tanks, the operational planning range was no more than 910 nautical miles. The calculation allowed for 36 gallons of fuel being used during warm up and take-off, engine revs. being a constant 2,300 r.p.m. (normal cruising), 50% of the flight endurance at heights up to 3,000 feet outbound and 50% at 15,000 feet inbound, with a drag effect of 5% for the protruding stores.

Interestingly, the work done by MAP caused them to allow 82 gallons for warm up and take-off. After allowing 25% of the remaining fuel as reserve, their studies came up with a range of 1,020 nautical miles. Additional wing tanks, in the form of drop tanks holding a total of 82 gallons, would extend the range to 1,177 nautical miles.

The constant engine speed of 2,300 rpm was dictated by engine and airframe peculiarities, which developed vibration in the coolant header tank if the revs. were lowered. Modifications to mount that header tank in flexible mountings would have to be made, which would allow the revs. to be cut back, at cruising speed, to 2,000; the effective range would increase by 80 nautical miles.

It had been decided that RAF Skitten would be the training base, and that the operation against the *Tirpitz*, codenamed *Servant*, would be launched from RAF Sumburgh, on the southernmost tip of the main Shetland Isle – the nearest UK base to Norway. The distance from Sumburgh to Trondheim was 550 miles, making a round trip of 1,100. So such an operation was feasible. The only trouble was that the *Tirpitz* had left Trondheim long ago and was in a fjord very much further north! If she remained where she was believed to be in March 1943, that target was 1,110 nautical miles from Sumburgh.

That problem – of how to get there and back again – was uppermost in everyone's thoughts. Between base and the target lay over 1,000 nautical miles of inhospitable seas – even in Spring and

Summer. The Germans would have, for certain, set up a fair amount of fire-power to defend its anchorage, and the more forewarning they had, the better their chances of knocking down Mosquitos. Then, after a successful attack, where do the aircraft make for?

"They're working on that," said Hutch dryly, without saying who "they" were. But whoever they were, they could not have been more preoccupied with the problem than we were in our isolated officers and sergeants messes at Skitten.

One of the briefing sessions was devoted to the details of the target itself – a study of the battle cruiser *Tirpitz*, and its sister ship the *Lutzow*.

Tirpitz was completed in July 1941, and was then the largest battleship ever built in Europe. She had a displacement of more than 50,000 tons and was 254 metres long overall. She carried a formidable armament, comprising eight 15-inch and twelve 5.9-inch long-range guns and eight torpedo tubes. She could thus stand-off from the lighter armament of the cruisers, destroyers and frigates that were providing escort to the Allied convoys. The traditional role of a battleship was to demolish the enemy's fighting ships in fairly close combat. But the *Tirpitz* was, instead, assigned the role of sea raider, whose primary targets would be merchant shipping. Her speed gave her the ability to hit hard and then to disappear into the oceans, or into her hiding places in the Norwegian fjords until it was time to prey on another convoy. She was also well able to defend herself against air attack, being equipped with sixteen 105 mm, sixteen 37 mm, and seventy eight 20 mm anti-aircraft guns – in all, one hundred and ten rapid fire guns capable of filling the sky with a blanket of flying steel and explosive. *Tirpitz* had slipped out undetected from the naval base at Kiel and steamed at full speed along the Norwegian coast, 'till turning in to the protection of Trondheim fjord. But, strangely, apart from a bombardment of the ice-free port of Spitzbergen on the edge of the ice cap, she had not fired her main armament by the time that 618 Squadron were putting together the plans for her destruction. She had moved from Trondheim to other fjords which had been made into fortresses by the occupying Germans. But, in any of these shelters, she would lie, like a fox in its lair, ready to make a sudden foray into the Atlantic to prey on the shipping lanes or on the Russian convoys. She was as much of a menace in her lair as she would have been prowling the oceans.

An attempt to destroy the *Tirpitz* had been made in the autumn of 1942 by the Royal Navy, and involving a very brave Norwegian fisherman, the legendary Leif Larsen, DSO, DSC, CGM, DSM*. Larsen was a skipper in the Shetland Bus Service, a clandestine operation in which trawlers and cutters were used to ferry men, materials and, most importantly, information in and out of Norway. He was put in command of a cutter, named the *Arthur*, which was loaded with peat for Trondheim. Concealed in that cargo were two two-man Chariot human torpedos, whose operators formed the *Arthur*'s crew. These human torpedos were so named because the crew of two sat astride the torpedo until it was primed and set on its run to the target, at which time the crew would seek to escape by a pre-planned route.

The *Arthur* was stopped for inspection by a German naval patrol at the entrance to Trondheim fjord – but the forged documents, and items like Norwegian magazines lying on the bunks, fooled the patrol and they were cleared to enter the fjord. There, the Chariots were quickly put overboard and under tow. The weather was foul, and tragedy struck when, less than five miles from *Tirpitz*, the towing cable snapped and the Chariots sank. Leif Larsen had no option than to scuttle the *Arthur*, and to make a getaway on foot. They were challenged by two German guards, and in the gunfight that immediately started, one of the sailors, A/S R. Evans, was wounded and had to be left behind, while the others made their way to Sweden and safety.[1]

The Russians had claimed that serious damage had been inflicted by one of its submarines on this German capital ship, but there was no evidence to support that claim.

One of 618 Squadron pilots who could talk from first hand experience of seeing one of the German capital ships was Jeffreys. In January 1943, Edmund Jeffreys, with his Observer Robert Irving on a reconnaissance operation while serving with 143 Squadron, North Coates, had located the *Scharnhorst* along the Norwegian coast. Jeffreys was awarded an immediate DFC.

[1] Larsen was in command of the Iceland trawler *Bergholm* in March 1943, which was attacked by JU88's. Some of the crew were killed, others including Larsen taking to a shattered lifeboat. They rowed to the shore over a period of several days. This may have been the incident on 1st March in which Hilliard, Hoyle, Turner and Curtis were involved while serving with 235 Squadron. They were despatched to the assistance of an escaping small vessel which was being bombed by JU88's. One of the JU88's was shot down by Sgt Vandewater of 235 Squadron.

In early May, the Commander-in-Chief, Coastal Command, went to RAF Medmenham to inspect the first three models of the target areas, the photographs of those models suggesting various approaches to the target, and the flak maps. He authorised that they be sent immediately to 618 Squadron, with the model of Langfjord to follow in the next few days.

Having learned something about the target, it was time to literally take the lid off the wooden packing cases that almost filled the floor of the Ops. Room. The first model, covering a floor area of about 12 feet by 12, was a very detailed layout of Kaa Fjord, and the ships at anchor. Kaa Fjord is an arm of the Alten Fjord, some 50 miles from Hammerfest, the most northerly town in the world. It lies well within the Arctic Circle in an area known as Finnmark. Hammerfest was a major U-boat base, and so was well defended. The fjords in the vicinity are very steep sided and with deep water close to the shore – ideal moorings for ships drawing about 50 feet of water. The *Scharnhorst* was anchored in nearby Langfjord for a time.

The climate in that Northern latitude is very changeable – even in summer, the sun might one day warm the air to 32°C, but then be followed by snow showers. From mid-May to the end of July the sun does not sink below the horizon at North Cape.

The Swedish border lies close-by to the east, and the Russian frontier was then less than 200 miles away around North Cape.

Hutch explained that the Germans had the capability of switching the capital ships in Langfjord and Kaa Fjord at very short notice, and, of course, there was always the risk that one of them would have slipped out, under cover of bad weather, into the Atlantic The weather conditions restricted the opportunites for high level photo reconnaissance by long-range Spitfires, which were not fired on – partly because their height afforded protection from ship and shore anti-aircraft fire, and partly because the Germans did not want to be drawing attention to the precise location of the battleship. Reconnaissance information from the Russians was not reliable, as most of it was dated by the time it was received. So, the planning had to work on assumptions on the precise location of the target, using last minute reconnaissance to give the final confirmation – if the weather allowed it.

In Kaa Fjord the usual mooring of the target was close into the western flank, lying fore and aft parallel to the coast. On the eastern side of the fjord was a finger of land, protruding from a spur which effectively split the fjord into two gorges. The attack would have to be made at 90° to the fore and aft line of the ship, which meant that there was precious little space to come down across that spur and finger to get into the straight and level attitude necessary before an effective release of the stores.

The approach from the sea would take the formation north of the fjord, near to Hammerfest, from where it would swing starboard to enter the mouth of the fjord. The lateral space between the slopes of the fjord was barely adequate for two waves of aircraft to make the turn through 180°, without serious risk of collision.

Following the release of the stores, each aircraft would have to climb sharply over the target and the steep slope of the fjord, to effect a rapid escape from the immediate vicinity.

The flak maps were then laid out alongside the models, as the briefing continued.

"This whole area is very heavily defended. There are other war-ships in that fjord, which will put up arcs of fire. On the shore, as you can see on the maps, there are flak batteries on the entrance to the fjord, on that spur and on the high ground looking over the fjord. These black blobs mark another feature – smoke pots. Smoke pots have been put in along the shore line, which in less than eight minutes can cover the whole area with a dense black smoke. If they have time to set these off before we make our runs, we might as well give up, because we'll probably not be able to see the target even at nought feet." Hutch was quietly spoken, and, realising that he had presented a pretty horrific picture in the last hour, he relaxed his features and smiled in that way that said: "Don't worry, it won't be as bad as that. We'll make it alright."

As the knowledge of what was going to be involved in Operation Servant increased, the crews started to be more and more aware of the isolation of their surroundings, and sometimes the desolation of the prospects of surviving this ordeal. The only people that a pilot or observer could talk to about the 'do' were others just like himself.

In spite of the strain that the aircrew were under, there was a very relaxed atmosphere within the camp, except when the station commander of RAF Wick was around. For instance, Sqn Ldr 'Tommy' Thomson, the Camp Commandant, carried his forage cap in his hand, a sign to passing junior officers, NCO's and other ranks that he did not wish to be saluted.

The camp cinema managed to put on a film once a fortnight. During one of the showings, at the end of April, the tannoy drowned out the sound from the film:– "Flight Sergeant Hilliard is to report to the Officers Mess immediately" Jimmy Hoyle, his observer, remarked in his Yorkshire accent: "You're getting a commission". No doubt in Jim's mind – if Hilly had been in trouble, it would have been an order to report to the adjutant. So the two of them walked back to the Sergeants Mess, where they downed a quick pint. They were joined by 'Fletch' Fletcher, who said that one of the officers had been over to look for Hilly. Another quick pint, and Hilly had enough Dutch courage to walk over to the Officers Mess.

At the door he was greeted by Des 'Chick' Curtis, who said: "Come in and meet the CO, Hilly, he's expecting you." Hutch gave a big welcoming grin, and said: "You're now a Pilot Officer." To the barman he called: "Give Pilot Officer Hilliard a pint, and give me a razor blade and the chalk. Better open a bar book for our new member, too." Hutch slit through the stitches holding the sergeant's stripes on Hilly's battle dress sleeves, then he chalked in the broad band of an air commodore. "You're my special guest tonight – that's why I have given you senior rank." Hilly vaguely remembers wandering into some barbed wire as he staggered back to his bunk many hours later.

Hilly and Jimmy were given three days' leave. They were flown down to RAF Leuchars in one of the old Beaufighters, so that Hilly could go to J. C. Smith, the gentleman's outfitters in St. Andrews, to be measured for his new uniform. That uniform was sent up to Hilly at Skitten in June 1943 – his barathea jacket and trousers cost the princely sum of eleven guineas, (£11.55 in decimal money) and his service dress hat £3.8s.6d, (£3.43). The total bill was £33.9s.5d and needed 105 clothing coupons.

Service tailors had to be very trusting in those wartime days, because the RAF Pay Office was not able to start paying newly-commissioned pilot officers from the day the commission was granted; often it was a couple of months before the first cheque, from either Glyn Mills or Lloyd's Cox & Kings bank, reached the officer.

While on the subject of service dress, Squadron Routine Orders in April spelled out that "Bundles of laundry are to be delivered to the Squadron Stores by 14.00 hours each Saturday. The items in the bundle must not exceed:–

Shirts	1
collars	3
vest	1
pants	1
socks	1 pair
handkerchiefs	3 pair"

That was the limit for airmen and airwomen alike. It's a good job that we all spent a lot of time in the fresh air!

Another notice in Squadron Routine Orders announced that a Special Leave Train was in service. Departing Wick at 16.30 on Sundays, it joined up with the train from Thurso – for naval personnel from Scapa Flow. It arrived in London, air raids permitting, late on Monday evening. The return was at 23.45 hours from London Euston on a Tuesday, arriving at Crewe at 04.35 hours Wednesday and reaching Wick at 00.09 hours on Thursday morning. Airmen returning from Newcastle-on-Tyne would catch the 05.40 hours to Carlisle and change to the train from Crewe. As a result of this 'improvement' in the service, leave travel time – the allowance that was added to the number of days' leave – was reduced from 48 to 24 hours. For someone whose home was in the West Country, most of a 7 day leave was spent travelling.

Once in a while one of the small travelling ENSA shows would put on their performance in the camp cinema/gymnasium, to provide some relief from the boredom. The officers and sergeants took turns to entertain the concert party after its show, and the performers were always put back into their coach in much higher spirits than when they arrived. The sergeants complained, though, that when it was their turn to act as hosts, if there were any passable looking girls in the ENSA team, the officers would invite themselves to join the Sergeants Mess party. But the Officers Mess was out of bounds to the NCO's. No justice. But there were few other diversions from the hi-jinks that went on in the mess.

The Assistant Camp Commandant and Officer i/c WAAF was a

young, attractive Section Officer, Barbara Bulloch. Other than when there were guests, she would be the only lady in the Officers Mess, a building so small that it did not rise to having a separate Ladies Lounge. We would all gather in the nissen hut, that was welded onto the breeze block entrance/dining hall, and which served as the bar. RAF dirty songs and some of the more violent games didn't get under way until Barbara sensed that her presence was no longer required – but she was such a good sport that this did not present any embarrassment. Most of the officers were accommodated in two blocks of rooms immediately facing the entrance to the mess; the rest were housed in a block that was part of the NCOs quarters. Barbara lived at one end of the officers quarters, sharing the access to that block. Hutch was great fun during the mess evenings, but he made it clear, just from his attitude, that ungentlemanly conduct towards Barbara would not be tolerated. There were evenings when she would relax over a drink or two. Then Hutch would assign one of the men to see her safely to her room, but that man had to be back in sight of Hutch very smartish – or have a good explanation.

Some of the fresh vegetables and eggs for the messes were supplied by a tradesman from Wick. His produce was always good and fresh and he soon had the entré to the Officers Mess bar. We had all noticed that he'd taken quite a shine to 'our' Barbara, but was getting too keen on plying her with more drinks than was good for her. Hutch tried to warn him off, but he was too thick to take the hint. There had been a lot of rain and the ground in front of the officers block was so muddy that duckboards were being used. On an evening, our local man was going a bit too far in his attentions to Barbara. Hutch spread the word around quietly that, if this civvy attempted anything with her, Hutch would sort him out! Soon, our local beau was walking Barbara from the mess and across into her quarters but he was not back in the bar quick enough. "Right, you two, go and fetch him, NOW" and they sped off while Hutch walked quietly to the front door of the mess. The somewhat shocked man was hauled out from where he had absolutely no right to be, and Hutch calmly crossed over, seized the man by his collar and flung him face-down into the mud. "I warned you to mind your manners. Now get out" said Hutch as, with a wry smile, he led us back to the bar to resume our drinking. We never fared quite so well for vegetables and eggs after that, but Hutch had made his point.

There was an awful drinking game that was played by the hour, and always ended with the victim becoming legless. It was called "Cardinal Puff", and it involved a 'candidate' being connned into believing that he could remember and repeat exactly what his mentor, across the table, would do and say. Every time the candidate got it wrong, he had to down a pint as a penalty. Those in the know were well aware that the candidate was going to lose, no matter how good his memory.

Across the table, the two men sat, each with a full pint. The mentor would pick up his pint, take a swig and say, "I drink to the health of Cardinal Puff for the first time", take another swig and put the mug back on the table. That was easy to follow. The next call would be to drink the cardinal's health for the second time, with two swigs each time – but the candidate would fail because he had, for example, picked up the glass with the wrong hand. The mentor then continued, adding more and more complications, and including vulgar deeds such as dipping a sock in the beer – with the candidate being, at the end, drunk and exhausted.

That would maybe last for an hour, then someone would suggest playing hi-cock-a-lorum or any of the other roughhouse games.

The CO of RAF Wick made a point of being present the first time that a dance was arranged in the station gymnasium down the road, and the next day, he admonished officers and NCO's for being unruly because they had been drinking beforehand – as if there was something unusual in that. The next time, knowing that he would be making an appearance, we hi-jacked the bus that was bringing WAAF up from the radar station south of Wick and from RAF Wick. After dropping off his passengers, the driver was invited to the Sergeants Mess for a drink – while the back of his bus was loaded with a couple of pins of beer and some bottles and glasses. He then gave us a lift to the dance, and, unbeknown to both him and the Station Commander, Wick, we had a lively party going on in the coach. Back in the gym, the CO called for silence, so that he could make his speech. We had to keep our feet on one of the officers who was a bit far gone, legless on the floor and who might have let the side down. But we were told how good it was to see that people could enjoy themselves without having to drink!

This all sounds pretty trivial, and perhaps suggests that these were the first 'lager louts' – but that would be a totally wrong impression and conclusion.

These were men in their twenties, some of them only 20 years old, highly trained and already battle-hardened, who were now working up to carry out an operation which would demand every skill and resource that they could muster, and even if it was highly successful, would probably cost most of them their lives. Football, volley ball and rugger worked off some of the energy – but there was no other way of trying to release pent-up emotional energy in that enclosed environment.

Charlie Rose came back from Manston with the news that further trials would be necessary, and Hutch announced that a target ship, a French warship the *Courbet,* was being anchored in Loch Striven, north of the mouth of the Clyde, on which some practise runs and drops would be made with inert stores.

These trials against the ship in Loch Striven would be conducted from RAF Turnberry, near Ayr, and the first of 618 Squadron ground crews were transferred there on 7th May. Hutch and the two flight commanders, Charlie Rose and Emjay Melville-Jackson, flew down there on 9th for two days of discussion and planning. The first five Mosquitos from Skitten were flown to Turnberry on 19th May. RAF Turnberry was a training airfield, and the same strict security cordon was thrown around the dispersal to which 618 Squadron was as-signed. So aircrews were spending part of the time at Turnberry and part at Skitten, with other non-operational flights as needed.

Those other aircraft movements were taking place all the time – as the aircraft required numerous modifications. For example, the wing roots had to be strengthened to take the additional weight of the wing drop-tanks, and the modification made to the coolant header tank. Some of these were carried out at Vickers, Weybridge and others at de Havilland, Hatfield.

These works visits came as a very welcome break from the Skitten/ Turnberry routines, as it gave some of the pilots and navigators the chance to get home to see wives and families, if only for a few hours. The hospitality extended by the directors of these factories was very generous. At Weybridge, for example, if an overnight stay was – hopefully – necessary, Vickers Armstrong paid for bed and break-fast in the Hand and Spear pub, that was just up the road towards Weybridge station from the factory. The pub was run by a dear old widowed lady, who made the aircrew very welcome, in spite of the pub having a very meagre beer ration. One evening, with the beer barrels empty and the bottled beer all drunk, someone espied the dear old lady sneaking off to bed with her bottle of Guiness. She was teased into believing that that precious bottle was going to be seized from her – and she was last seen scurrying through the kitchen in her bedroom slippers and woolly dressing gown, clutching the precious bottle to her bosom.

At Hatfield, the famous Comet Hotel was the drinking well. It was not unusual to meet (Sir) Geoffrey de Havilland and the de Havilland test pilots in the bar there – and that was a great chance to learn from their experience of flying the Wooden Wonder. (Later on, in August, Turner, Curtis, Hilliard and Hoyle were in the bar of the Comet in the company of Sir Geoffrey de Havilland when one of the directors came in, looking very sad. He had the job of telling Sir Geoffrey that his son, John, had just been killed when two Mosquitos had collided as they completed test flights close to the airfield.)

On 13th May, DZ535, with Sgts Ellis and Donald aboard, swung on take-off at Skitten; the undercarriage collapsed and the aircraft was wrecked, fortunately without injury to the crew. Johnny Walker and Leon Murray were taking off from Turnberry, when the aircraft swung and continued on through 90°. They missed the lighthouse on the shore-edge by a whisker.

Wg Cdr Hutchinson and his observer Flg Off Francis French, had been at Weybridge in DZ493, and were setting off to deliver that aircraft to Turnberry on 17th May 1943. The aircraft swung violently as it unstuck, was briefly airborne, then turned steeply, still only feet from the ground. It touched a vehicle on the perimeter track, then hit a lorry and a van, then crashed into a barrage balloon cable. The aircraft burst into flames, but miraculously, both crew members got out, Hutch being slightly injured. While he was still recovering from these injuries, news came through that he had been awarded a DFC for gallantry while serving in command of 235 Beaufighter Squadron. On 27th May Wg Cdr J. M. N. 'Jumbo' Pike, DSO, DFC came up from Headquarters, Coastal Command to act as commanding officer. He had been involved in the planning of this Operation *Servant*, and so was an excellent choice as acting CO.

On 20th May, three days after Hutch's accident, two other aircraft were coming in to land at Weybridge – DZ529 and DZ547. DZ547, piloted by Flt Lt Jeffreys DFC, struck a van on the perimeter track as he came over the threshold, writing off the aircraft and injuring his passenger, Sgt Coleman, and one civilian on the ground.

Mosquito DZ465 was found to have a cracked bulkhead, and was put into Cat AO unworthiness, then DZ423 also was found to have a cracked No 7 bulkhead, and was declared un-airworthy in Cat AC.

Of the Mosquitos lent by RAF Marham, DZ468 had crashed at North Coates on 16th April, DZ486 had crashed at Durness on 5th April, DZ489, DZ355 and DZ293 were returned on 20th May, DZ518 was repaired and returned on 2nd June, DZ465 on 21st June and DZ423 on 19th July.

On 17th May 618 Squadron heard on the mess radio that Bomber Command had carried out a massive low level attack on the Möhne and Eder Dams in the Ruhr valley, with catastrophic effects on the German war industries. There was no description of the 'mine' that was used, so there was no reason to assume that there was any direct connection between that raid and the work of 618 Squadron. But the original target date had passed, and no new date was given for the attack on the *Tirpitz*.

The dropping trials on Loch Striven continued, then, on one late morning flight, with an array of senior RAF and Naval officers, and their senior civil servants on board the *Courbet*, one of the stores was released under ideal conditions. It bounced exactly as it should, losing height with each skip, and keeping a straight track to its target. But, it was in the middle of one of its skips when it hit the side of the ship, and, instead of spinning down the hull into the protective net, it tore a neat hole through the bow. There was a frantic rush of top brass into whatever shelter they could find. Red Very lights were flashed off in all directions, to stop any further drops. The Mossie crew and the other crews that were waiting their turn were still chuckling as they climbed from their aircraft back at Turnberry.

At that time of the year, sunset was very late at Skitten – so there was always plenty of daylight if one felt energetic enough for a walk round the perimeter track after dinner. On one such evening, a couple of aircrew were walking the perimeter track. Flying had finished for the day, so the airfield and tower were closed. To the north-east they saw a heavy aircraft, larger than anything based at Wick, on a south-east heading at about 2,000 feet. This was unusual, so they stopped to watch it pass; but, instead, it began a shallow turn westwards. A Liberator with USAAF markings was going to come in at Skitten. Sure enough, it made a gentle landing and taxied round to the deserted control tower. Out jumped one of the crew, in a leather Irvine jacket, and with headphones over his crushed peaked cap.

"Are you English?" he asked.

"Of course," Such a stupid question to ask of three RAF officers in battledress.

"What's this place called?"

"The north of Scotland," Doug Turner told him, cautiously.

"Thank God" He called to the rest of the crew to climb out.

They were walked them across to the Officers Mess, and the Sergeants Mess was told that they also had a couple of visitors.

Over a drink, while a meal was being rustled up, the captain related how they were in transit from the United States, via Newfoundland, Iceland and Prestwick, to join a squadron in the South of England. Soon after taking off from Rekjavik in Iceland the radio compass had packed in. For some inexplicable reason, they didn't return to the transit base in Iceland and the aircraft didn't appear to have a standard magnetic compass, so the captain had "pointed the machine in the direction of Britain", and they had continued the flight. By good fortune, their track had taken them through the Pentland Firth, and they had seen the mainland on the starboard side. Somehow they had not seen RAF Wick, which they must have passed almost overhead.

The crew seemed nonplussed when it was explained that, had their track taken them a bit more northerly, they would have arrived unannounced and without flight clearance over Scapa Flow; and the Royal Navy would have ended their service in Europe.

They were shown a set of ordnance survey maps covering the route from Skitten to Prestwick, and given map reading instructions:–

"You turn right (avoiding difficulties like 'port' and 'starboard') and stay with the coastline at about 1,500 feet. You'll see the inlet of Dornoch Firth, but a gentle left turn takes you in sight of Inverness. On the west side of Inverness you see the canal and the long narrow water of Loch Ness. Keep going over the loch, and over other lochs until you come to open sea. Bear left keeping in sight of the mainland. Then call Prestwick for a QDM and you'll be on a course of about

120 to take you to the airfield. The weather forecast is good, so it's a good sightseeing run".

They were not convinced of the simplicity of this flight, so one of 618's navigators flew with them, involving a wasted morning having to fly a Mosquito to Prestwick to bring the navigator back. Doubtless they would have been amazed had they learnt anything about the operation that was being planning, and the high degree of navigational accuracy that was called for.

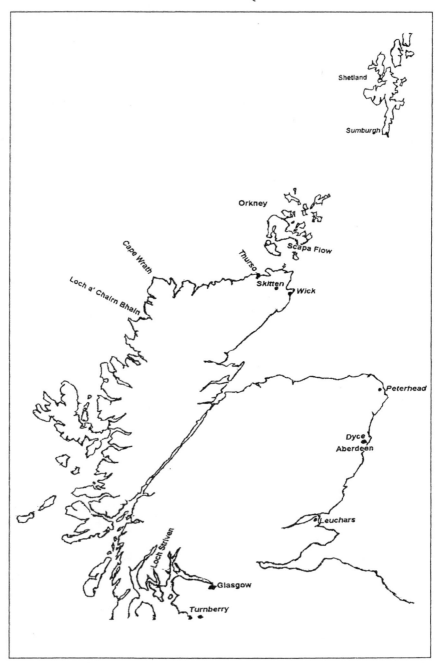

Map of Scotland showing the RAF airfields of Skitten and Turnberry, and the Lochs used by 618 Squadron for Highball practice.

CHAPTER 5

The War Lords Deliberate

The urgency to develop practical versions of the 'bouncing bomb' and the production of aircraft types in which to carry them had dominated the minds of the senior naval and air force officers during February and into March 1943. The critical date of not later than 26th May was too close for comfort.

On 17th March 1943 the War Cabinet listed the Priority Strategic Targets[1] as:–
  a) Anti U-boat – shelters, lock gates, U-boats, against dockyard walls.
  b) "Husky", e.g. Italian heavy ships at sea or in harbour, and dams.
  c) Bombing Germany, e.g. Ruhr dams.
  d) Heavy units of German Fleet.
  e) German transport – shipping, bridges, locks, dams in waterways.
  f) War against Japan – fleet and ships in harbour.
  g) Cross Channel – dams, inland waterways.

At that time, the Allies were driving the Germans from North African, and plans were well under way for the invasion of Sicily in July 1943. It is not surprising therefore that a higher priority was given to the Italian fleet, most of which was based at Taranto in the 'instep' of the heel of Italy, than to the Ruhr dams and the destruction of the *Tirpitz*. The Chiefs of Staff – Naval and Air Force – had participated in drawing up this list of priority strategic targets, and now it was time to assess the feasibility of applying this priority.

On 24th March, Air Marshal Jack Slessor, the Commander-in-Chief, Coastal Command had received insructions to form a new Mosquito squadron. The following day he had taken part in the meeting in Whitehall that reviewed developments in the operations involving both the *Upkeep* and *Highball* weapons. He had heard that, because the *Tirpitz* was then lying beyond the normal operational range of Mosquito aircraft, the Mosquito squadron, which he was

---

[1] (PRO AIR 20 2617)

about to form, could be lost within 90 days of its formation. On 27th March he received a letter from the Asst Chief of Air Staff (Ops), Air Vice Marshal Norman Bottomley, relaying some difficult questions that had been posed by the Chief of Naval Staff.

He was asked to decide what numbers of aircraft could be made available by 'the ultimate date of employment', and what number of ships which may have to be attacked, adding that, for certain Italian ports, aircraft would have to be based temporarily overseas. "Would you comment on what period might be assumed as necessary for the training of crews: a) for conversion, and b) for technical training to fit them for a particular operation." Even the wording of the questions was difficult.

Jack Slessor replied, on 29th March:– "We know extremely little about the weapon and I have very little experience of converting crews to Mosquito. Anything I say can therefore be, at best, a more or less intelligent guess. We have not even got to the stage of making a tactical plan for the attack on the major units at Narvik. [*Tirpitz* or *Lutzow*] On the assumption, however, that the weapon will do all that is claimed for it and that it turns out, as I think it should, to be fairly easy to get a goodish proportion of hits on big ships, releasing at about 1,500 yards, I should say that the minimum forces that we should provide for the objectives listed are as follows:–

– for the German heavy ships in Narvik, one squadron of 20 aircraft,

– for the *Graf Zeppelin*, on the assumption that she is somewhere where we can get at her with a reasonable chance of success and without prohibitive loss, one flight of 10 aircraft,

– for the Italian heavy ships, one squadron of 20 aircraft.

"This means raising and training two and a half squadrons, each of 20 aircraft. I reckon it is going to take us the full time to get one squadron converted and adequately trained by the 26th May. i.e. two months from the word 'Go'. This is taking a picked Wing Commander, and two picked squadron leaders, 8 picked Beaufighter crews, and 9 Mosquito bomber experienced crews. You can't raise two and a half squadrons that way without wrecking 2 Group and making very serious holes – to put it mildly – in my Beaufighter squadrons. If you are prepared to do that, then I have no doubt that you could get your two and a half squadrons trained in two months each. So the date that they would all be trained would depend on the rate of supply of Mosquitos. I don't say that it would not be worth it;

indeed if we could be reasonably sure of putting all these heavy ships in the bag it would be worth it. In fact, I think you've got to do it that way if you do it at all.

"It isn't worth just taking any old squadron with its usual ration of Pilot Officer Prunes and re-equipping them with Mosquitos, and arming it with this potentially decisive weapon.

"The whole thing seems to me to depend on whether this weapon really would sink a heavy ship. If it will, then I think that we shall do, though I daresay it will be a costly operation.

"Two minor points that you have no doubt thought of. If this operation is postponed, security will suffer. We will do our best to keep it dark, but you know what it is if you try to keep this sort of thing secret too long; someone is bound to leak and speculation will be rife among those not in on the secret. If we do not pull it off on the stated date and we have to keep the chaps in training, we shall want more inert *Highballs*."

The point had been made there about the importance of the element of surprise, and the associated need for complete secrecy. But, of course, the wider the scope and the greater the complications of the 'bouncing bomb' projects the larger the number of people who would get to know. The Chief of the Air Staff, Charles (later Lord) Portal, took a very personal interest in the security aspect. In March 1943 he sent a rocket to Norman Bottomley, asking if special orders about Security had been issued. He commented, regarding a letter he had received from Bottomley, that it should have been addressed "Personally to the C-in-C and to the CAS and to ACAS' only" and on the principle that it should not be handled or seen by anyone except officers who MUST know about it.

The highly secret nature of this weapon caused the subject to be excluded from the Minutes of the meetings of the Chiefs of Staff of the Air and Naval Forces. An important source of research information is, therefore, the papers that were put to the Chiefs of Staff for discussion at those meetings.

The comments by the CAS probably stimulated the Director of Intelligence (Security) into writing a memo to the Chief and Assistant Chiefs of Air Staff that gave the cover story to be used among those who would, in some ways, be involved with the project:–

"The weapon is a special type of mine and the wooden casing surrounding it is provided for protection in handling. This is particularly necessary as the mine is designed for use in localities where it will be handled by native labour. The spinning device is in connection with the fusing, which is effected by centrifugal action. The uses of the weapon are, in the main, anti-submarine but it will also function against shipping.

"Units armed with the weapon are to be known as Special Mining Squadrons."[2]

The operations planners and chiefs of staff intended that, on the date designated for the attack on the Ruhr dams, there would be simultaneous attacks on the *Tirpitz* and on the Italian capital ships in Taranto harbour. The Ministry of Aircraft Production had ordered 30 modified Mosquitos Mk IV, unarmed bomber version, for 618 Squadron, but had told de Havilland to 'pencil in' a probable allocation of a similar, additional, number. The War Cabinet Chiefs of Staff Committee was told, in a paper dated 3rd April 1943, that these modified aircraft were coming off the production line at the rate of 5 per week; the first 16 to be completed by 8th May, and total order to be completed "about the end of May". There were 20 air crews on 618 Squadron, so the minimum number of aircraft had to be 20 on the day of the attack, assuming no wastage or unserviceability. The production rate could not achieve that number by the planned date of 15th May.

The additional 30 aircraft could be provided by the middle of July 1943, by which time that Mark IV version was to go out of production. If, thereafter, any more of these modified aircraft were needed – for instance to replace losses through crashes – they would have to be made from either the Mark IX or the fighter/bomber version Mark VI – but in either case, the modifications would be so extensive that the cost and the disruption to production would be very high. If any numbers were needed, they would have to be introduced onto the production line, with a lead time of at least four months. So the finite number – for 1943 – of the *Highball* aircraft would be 60.[3]

A meeting at the Admiralty, attended also by Air Ministry and RAF senior officers, on 5th April had, as its primary purpose, the formulation of possible plans for the employment of *Highball* against naval targets, so that these plans would be ready in the event that the weapon proved a success. The Admiralty accepted responsibility for

[2] PRO AIR 6-63 and AIR 20-2617
[3] PRO AIR 15-442

stating the order of priority of naval targets, the Chief of Staff would allocate priority of aircraft, and the C-in-C Coastal Command would determine the scale of effort required and the tactical feasibility of carrying out the attack.

Intelligence staffs were working out if it would be possible to delay Operation *Chastise* (the attack on the dams) for about a month. This would give time for Coastal Command to build up a bigger force and thereby increase the size of the initial blow.

Admiral Renouf said that his committee had advised the Chiefs of Staff that they did not think that the attack on the Italian fleet could be carried out for some time without accepting the risks imposed by flying the aircraft direct to the target or via Gibraltar and North Africa, with the consequent risk of compromising security.

Jack Slessor had made the point to that War Cabinet Chiefs of Staff Committee that an operation against ships in Taranto harbour would have to be carried out from either Malta or North Africa. The direct route from the UK posed real problems of security in the event that an aircraft had to force-land whilst still armed. The modified *Highball* aircraft did not have sufficient range to assure the flight from Portreath in Cornwall to Gibraltar, and head winds or adverse weather could cause losses due to forced landing at sea. If the squadron was obliged to wait for favourable winds and weather for the first leg of the flight, no date could be set for the attack.

The alternative would be to ship the aircraft, knocked down, then re-erect them in the Mediterranean area – a task that would take months to achieve and would require De Havilland and Vickers sending skilled workers to accompany the aircraft. Those workers could only be made available at considerable cost in terms of lost production. The committee also had in mind the ending of the Mosquito Mark IV production run.

The point was made that the effective cost of providing these two and a half squadrons would be at the expense of Bomber Command. Thirty aircraft would normally meet the wastage of the 2 day-bomber squadrons of No 2 Group and the Oboe squadron of Pathfinder Force. They would also have been providing the resources for the Oboe Repeater Unit, which was then being formed on high priority to develop the Oboe Repeater System. Withholding 30 aircraft, in addition to those 30 already in the process of conversion, would not allow MAP to meet wastage in any of the three Bomber Command Mosquito squadrons [Nos. 105, 109 and

139 Squadrons] or of providing the 8 Mosquitos required for the Oboe Repeater Unit.

There was also the important matter of availablility of crews. The Bomber Command crews would have to undertake the conversion and training of more Coastal Command Beaufighter crews, which could render 2 day-bomber squadrons temporarily ineffective, at a time when those squadrons were proving so effective in making precision attacks. Equally, the Beaufighter squadrons of Coastal Command would be very seriously weakened by the abrupt withdrawal of these skilled crews.

Norman Bottomley had added his comment, that the provision of the 30 aircraft for 618 Squadron had already prevented the re-equipment with Mosquitos of No 305 Polish Squadron, in spite of a pledge given to the Polish Government in exile less than a month earlier at the Chiefs of Staff level.

In the previous chapter we have noted that, at the meeting on 5th April at the Admiralty, the real problems of mounting an atack on the Italian capital ships at Taranto had been spelled out. The magnitude of those problems led those present to believe that the project would be abandoned, and the task assigned to American day-bombing squadrons.

Yet, on 24th May, the War Cabinet agreed to proceed as a matter of urgency with plans for *Highball* attacks on Italian capital ships, following which, on 4th June, a signal went from ACAS (Ops) to the Commander-in-Chief, Mediterranean Command informing him that Air Commodore Vasse would be arriving to explain Operations *Chastise*, using *Upkeep*, and *Servant*, using *Highball*. A complete back-up of a unit equipped with sufficient spares for 2 months' operations of the Mosquito Mark IV B was being sent by a special ship that was sailing on 10th June. Key personnel and other equipment would be flown out when the operational decision was made. The signal concluded that "We propose to send an officer of 618 Squadron to discuss details of the planning". The possibility of an attack on the Italian fleet was still on the agenda at the end of June 1943. But none of 618 Squadron aircrew recall an officer being sent to the Mediterranean war zone, nor is there any record of the equipment being shipped.

It was, perhaps, strange that the aircrew of 618 Squadron were told on their first aquaintance with Operation *Servant* that the target date was 15th May. It could have been a straightforward error – as the C-in-C had already used the date of 26th May in his correspondence.

The determining factors were, firstly, the short period of time when conditions would be right for the attack on the Ruhr dams, which has already been referred to in Chapter 3. The very last day , if the attack was to be made in 1943, was 26th May. Given all that had to be achieved from the time that the directive to form these squadrons was issued, it is probable that the date of 15th May was used to implant in everyone's mind the urgency of getting things done.

The other factor was the initial supposition that the 617 and 618 Squadron attacks had to be simultaneous – to preclude the Germans discovering the nature of the weapon and putting in countermeasures between the attacks. If the dams raid took place first, and one of the bombs or stores failed to detonate and was recovered, or even if it came to rest on land or in a crashed aircraft, the Germans could quickly assess what had caused the bomb to clear the protective booms, and alert other possible target locations. The attack would be made in moonlight, with the probability that some Germans would see the bombs skipping across the still waters of the lakes.

There was no possibility of the Mosquito raid taking place ahead of that of the Lancasters, because the aircraft production rate would not allow that. Hence the pleading from those concerned with Operation *Servant* for more time.

These comments about operational squadrons being deprived of sorely needed replacements provided ammunition to the sceptics, who were able to point out also that the weapon – in both the *Upkeep* and the *Highball* forms – had not proved itself to be the sure-fire success that had earlier been suggested.

One of the tests to which these stores was subjected was that of full speed spinning of the stores loaded with HE and with detonators. The purpose of these tests was to determine if the centrifugal force applied by the spin to the cylinder containing the explosive would cause the charge to move, or to create the risk of premature explosion. These tests took place in Richmond Park, west of London during the period from 26th April to 10th May. No doubt the rigs were hidden from public view in the park, and the inquisitive golfers and dog walkers were probably told that the Bomb Disposal Unit was digging up an unexploded land mine.

The larger store for Operation *Upkeep* was having problems, in that the wooden outer casing would not withstand the impacts of hitting the water, during continued trials at Reculver. On Sunday 18th April, Barnes Wallis and Professor Taylor were watching the releases, and saw that after the casing broke on one store, it carried on bouncing in a straight line. They immediately ordered the casing to be removed from the next inert stores and later that day, watched as the new shape – a simple cylinder – performed almost exactly as Barnes Wallis had originally predicted. The decision was immediately taken to make the cylinder the shape for the operational version of *Upkeep*.

General Ismay, and the Chiefs of Staff were advised in a memo dated 13th May[4] that the cylindrical form and the fittings gave no indication of the method of release or the surface running principle. The very short range of run – of 450 yards including the air path – and the method of attack might well engender the belief that a special form of depth charge had been dropped between the boom and the dam. This belief might be confirmed by the attack on the Sorpe Dam in which an aircraft would fly close and parallel to the dam face, Bounces at this short range closely resemble the normal skip effect when a bomb is dropped short of target.

It was thought highly improbable that the Germans would associate *Upkeep* with the principle of a spherical weapon suitable for use against ships, where long range is essential. There was the risk that the spinning principle might be disclosed if an aircraft was shot down in enemy territory, but the danger of associating this attack with its use as an anti-shipping weapon was considerably reduced, and that risk should be accepted.

The Chiefs of Staff were told that the water levels in the dams were satisfactory for this mode of attack, that the 23 Lancasters that were "frozen" for this attack were badly needed for normal bombing operations, the weapon had one more test – that day – and the crews had reached their peak of training. On the other hand, the trials of *Highball* against the *Courbet* were revealing that the velocity at

4 PRO AIR 6-63 and AIR 20-2617

the point of striking were critical – a polite way of referring to the hole made in the bows of this ship. The crews of 618 Squadron needed considerable further training before *Highball* could be used. The likelihood of devastating results from the Ruhr dams raids and the greatly reduced risk of prejudicing the future *Servant* operation suggested that authority to go ahead immediately with Operation *Chastise* should be given. The Chiefs of Staff gave that Go Ahead with effect from 14th May and the attacks were made on the night of 16/17th May.

The timing of the attack on the *Tirpitz* would now depend on solving the technical problems of the store, and the development of practicable tactics for the attack and recovery.

A working committe had been set up by the Chiefs of Staff to review fortnightly the progress being made in resolving the technical problems of the weapon, the delivery of aircraft and the modifications that had to be made, and of the tactical problems.

It was told that, on 5th May, a conference was held at MAP to discuss the new 3/8th″ steel plating that would cover the store. Trials of this new model would begin from Turnberry as soon as the squadron Armaments Officer had completed balancing the stores, preparing the depth charge and self-destructing pistols and loading the aircraft.

Those trials would be staged with the aircraft flying at 50 to 60 feet, at a ground speed of 360 knots, with the stores spinning at 700 rpm. The first stores would be released at a range of 1,200 yards, but the range would then be altered to suit the results being observed. The depth charge pistols, normally set to fire at 27 feet, could be made to function at 40 feet by fitting springs.

The main particpant in those trials was Charlie Rose, in which 10 stores were released against the *Courbet*. Five of the stores were lost due to mechanical problems in the release gear. On one drop, the store hit the ship on its third bounce at approximately 5′ 6″ above the water line. On another drop, the store made a normal run, and on its second bounce made impact with the side of the ship at approximately 11′ 6″ above the water line at a very high striking velocity. (This caused the scattering of the VIP observers, that gave the aircrews so much amusement).

The hydrophones on board did not detect any proper functioning of the detonating pistols.

Further trials against the *Courbet* took place on 17th, 18th and 22nd May.

On the day before the use of the *Upkeep* cylindrical stores against the Ruhr dams, an important meeting took place at Vickers, Weybridge. Vickers were represented by Dr Barnes Wallis and its two test pilots, Captain Mutt Summers and Sqn Ldr 'Shorty' Longbottom, Wg Cdrs Ker and Pike from HQCC, and Wg Cdr Hutchinson and Sqn Ldrs Rose and Melville-Jackson of 618 Squadron. This was very much a review session, following the failures of the *Highball* drops against the *Courbet* earlier in May.

One of the causes of the failures was that the marker buoy that should have been positioned 1,200 yards out from the ship – to mark the release point – had been incorrectly positioned at 800 yards. The result was that the store had lost little of its forward velocity, and the high striking velocity, at the point of impact, had shown that the store itself suffered severe damage and the detonating pistol was not able to withstand that impact. Much negative information had been learned from this set of drops, and, on the positive side, only that the pilot would be able to achieve considerable accuracy in the direction of the drop.

As previously noted, there were also failures in the release mechanism in the bomb bay. Barnes Wallis had also discovered that there were variations in the dimensions of the stores after they had been filled, and errors in the jigs that were used for setting up the caliper arms. Vickers were going to make some new gauges for both the inert and high explosive stores.

After a further set of trials at Manston by Shorty Longbottom and Charlie Rose, which would include a 30 minute spinning endurance test at 1,000 rpm, the aircraft would return to Turnberry for the next trials in Loch Striven.

The dropping range would initially be 1,600 yards, at 360 mph, with the store spinning at 900 to 1,000 rpm; the release height would be 50-60 feet. Then, assuming success, the range would be decreased in steps of 200 yards until the hydrostatic pistol and timing system failed. Then, the range would be increased to determine the maximum range.

Hutch had stressed the importance of knowing the maximum and minimum ranges, even though the maximum may not be feasible within the fjord. Barnes Wallis said that if the RAF wanted a minimum range in calm water as short as 800 yards, the store as presently engineered would not withstand the force of impact at a high release speed. That would entail redesigning the store with a very much reduced charge-to-weight ratio; that modification would involve more delay in producing the operational version.

Barnes Wallis was producing a new range finder which could be set by the pilot to suit smooth or rough water. The inert stores had not been tested in rough water, but it was estimated that the range would reduce by as much as 20%.

The 'flattened' sides of the stores looked similar from the outside, with the attendant risk that they could be incorrectly loaded into the bomb bays. Instructions were being given to the munitions factory that each store had to be marked in red on the pistol end with the loose ring nut, for loading to port. The self-destruction pistol end would be marked green and loaded to starboard.

A status report on 13th May gives some idea of the state of preparedness of aircraft and weaponry:–

- 6 Mosquitos delivered to 618 Squadron, Skitten, but have still to return to de Havillands for fitting long-range tanks;
- 12 at de Havillands for long-range tank fitting;
- 1 on the trials at Manston.
- VHF had been fitted at Vickers into 18 aircraft;
- 99 High Explosive HE stores had been made, of which 40 were being sent to RAF Sumburgh;
- 104 Inert stores made, of which 60 were shipped to Turnberry, 20 to Manston and 24 were in the course of being plated;
- 17 more inert stores were en route to the filling station.

This was a very satisfactory production rate for the stores, given the uncertainties of performance and the frequent changes in design that ensued.

The 99 HE stores at Sumburgh would be more than sufficient for the 20 aircraft to be used in the attack.

The trials had concentrated on releasing a single store. The optimum results were being achieved with the aircraft flying at 360 mph at a height of 30 to 50 feet above the water, with release being made at ranges of 1,000 to 1,400 yards when attacking a ship at an angle of approach of between 45° and 60°. But during the months of June and July, problems continued to occur in the running of the store. What was happening was that the balancing weights had moved slightly, causing the store to adopt an elbowing motion which, in turn, altered the axis of rotation.

The two stores, loaded in tandem in the bomb bay, could not be released simultaneously, as they could collide on first hitting the sea, particularly in rough water. The trailing store would be upset by the slipstream and the wave patterns formed by the leading store. So the release mechanism was being adjusted to give a time interval of 2 to 3 seconds, so that there was an adequate spacing between the bombs en route to the target.

During May and June, the aircrews were mostly employed in ferrying the aircraft. Continued practise at low level flying over the sea was non-productive, as this did not require too much skill as a training exercise devoid of the tension of flying into hostile waters and the impending attack. There had not been any opportunity for the full squadron to fly off for a mock attack, as there was not a time when the squadron was at full strength on one airfield.

CHAPTER 6

Overcoming Distance

Barnes Wallis and the technical experts were feverishly working to eliminate the problems of *Highball* stores. It would be intolerable for the crews of 618 Squadron to deliver these stores on their way to the target, only to have them fail to destroy the *Tirpitz*.

To the aircrew, the more pressing matter was the distance that separated Sumburgh, in the Shetlands, from where the *Tirpitz* was at anchor. They had no right to see the memos that were passing between the service chiefs and their advisers, containing phrases such as: "... would involve the possible loss of all aircraft". These were experienced crews, who could make their own evaluations – and the evaluations that they were making suggested to them that the powers that be didn't have any of the right answers to the simple question: "How do we avoid losing all the crews during or after the attack?" The aircrew went about their work from Skitten or Turnberry, but they were not able to talk to anyone except other crews about their concerns or opinions. It was a lonely environment in which to be caged for weeks on end.

Naval and RAF navigation officers in Command Headquarters had been working on the distances involved from Sumburgh to possible target locations. A memo dated 7th April 1943,[1] which, interestingly, began with the comment that Operation *Servant* might be postponed until the end of June, noted that Intelligence considered that Altenfjord and Narvik were the most likely anchorages to be used by the Germans in the next two months. Trondheim, within easy reach of Sumburgh, was ruled out as most unlikely.

SUMBURGH to ALTENFJORD and KAAFJORD and return was 1,800 n.ms. SUMBURGH to NARVIK and return was 1,430 n.ms.

Operational trials had not then been completed to determine the

---

[1] PRO AIR 15-442 Doc 29A

endurance of the *Highball* Mosquito, but with a flight plan that required a zero to 3,000 feet altitude on the outward leg and a climb to 15,000 feet, stores gone, on the return, the range of the Mosquito without drop tanks would be 912 n.ms.

So, at the first look, the Mosquitos could not reach the anticipated target areas, let alone return. That pointed to the need to fit drop-tanks, which would automatically trigger a delay in the date by which the operation could be mounted. De Havilland gave, as their first estimate, a time of one month per aircraft to manufacture and fit these drop-tanks. The extra fuel in the 100 gallon tanks would enable the aircraft to make the attack, but not to make the return journey.

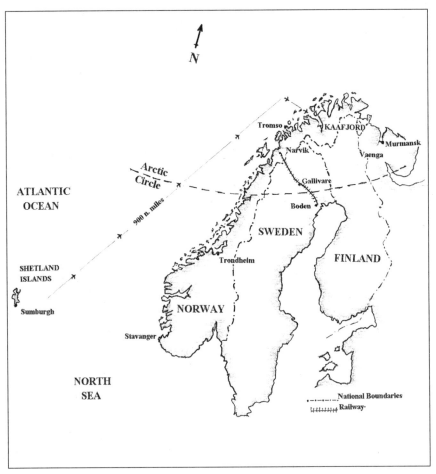

Map showing relative positions of Sumburgh Airfield to the Tirpitz *anchorage in Kaa Fjord.*

An alternative, discussed in that memo, would be to embark the squadron on an aircraft carrier, from which the aircraft could be flown off within range of the *Tirpitz*. There were some snags to this scheme.

The aircraft would have to be dis-sembled prior to embarkation, and eight skilled men from the manufacturers would have to be available during the passage northwards – to re-assemble the 20 aircraft. The aircraft would be then air tested by flying off for the attack!

No-one had any experience of flying off twin-engined aircraft – let alone types with a wing span of 54 feet. Trials would have to be conducted by test pilots, on a carrier which the Royal Navy would have to withdraw from active service. Even it proved practicable to fly off Mosquitos, several months would have to be set aside to train 618 Squadron aircrews.

There could be problems of being ready on time if any of the de Havilland/Vickers men or the aircrew suffered sea-sickness during this voyage. Those aircraft carriers were not fitted with stabilisers, and heavy North Atlantic seas could lay low even the most stalwart landlubber. The Royal Navy raised the critical matter of an accident occurring during take-off. Suppose one of the aircraft slipped over the side or over the bows, the detonation of the hydrostatic *Highball* fuses in the stores might well destroy the carrier – with probable heavy losses, and the operation having to be abandoned.

That idea didn't seem to have too much to commend it to the planners. The next one filled the aircrew with horror when they were told that it was even put up as an idea, let alone that it was being studied.

This was that the Mosquitos, fitted with drop-tanks to enable them to get to the target, should then come back into the North Atlantic and rendezvous over a British ship. The aircrew would bale out over the ship – the type of ship and its size were not specified – and the ship would then pick them up. Let us assume that, by some miracle, all 40 aircrew made it safely away from the target and onto the rendezvous, The aircrew could decide to bale out one aircraft at a time, damaged and injured first. The ship would launch small boats which, in heavy seas, would scurry around trying to find the crews in the water. Of course, in heavy seas with maybe 15 foot waves, if the sailors in the rescue boats didn't spot where the parachutes hit the sea, they probably wouldn't spot the men floating in their Mae Wests. Even in early summer, the sea water would be bitterly cold, and the exhausted airmen could not be expected to survive more than a couple of minutes of immersion. It might be better to suffer the quick death of being shot down by the *Tirpitz* or the covering flak. Some of us from Coastal Command were all too aware, also, that the Royal Navy would not stop engines while the rescue went on, with the risk of being torpedoed by U-boats that traversed that area.

Depending on where the target was anchored, the Swedish border was only a few hundred miles away so why not tell the aircrew to fly into neutral Sweden and either crash land or bale out? There was a railway line from Narvik, running south east through Gellivare to Boden, inland at the top of the Gulf of Bothnia. With typical English understatement, the memo comments:— "Owing to the thickly wooded and mountainous nature of the country this would be at best a hazardous enterprise." If the attack was made in Altenfjord or Kaa Fjord, the escaping aircraft would then either have to turn out to sea and turn inland again further south, to cross the defended area of Narvik in search of the rail line, or to fly south across the barren highlands of Lappland and hope to catch sight of the rail track as they crossed it. Those who survived the crash landing and be lucky enough to be rescued would then be interned in Sweden for the duration of hostilities.

The next idea was that if the attack took place in Altenfjord, the surviving aircraft should make for the Russian airfield at Vaenga. The location of that airfield was known to the West as it had been used previously by Hampdens and Spitfires.

But the memo qualifies that idea, saying that "the chances of reaching Vaenga after the attack depend entirely upon a favourable surface wind. Nor are the chances of reaching even the most desolate parts of Swedish territory appreciably better than those of reaching Russia." The calculated distance from Sumburgh to Narvik and on to Vaenga was 1,060 n.ms. The distance if the target was in Altenfjord was 1,110 n.ms. Neither of these distances left any room for manoeuvre, even with drop-tanks fitted.

The author of the memo. went on to consider the option of removing one of the stores and replacing it with an easily demountable fuel-tank, which would give the aircraft a theoretical range of 1,180 n.ms. That would reduce the effectiveness of the attack by 50%, so reducing the chances of success.

When the aircrew were told of the possibility of flying into a Russian airfield, their immediate question was: "That's fine. But how do we get out from there?" Wg Cdr Pike, on a visit from HQCC, fielded that question.

"The situation with the Russians is not too easy at the moment. Probably the Russians will want to take the aircraft for their own use, so we are considering the idea of a British cruiser going into Murmansk, and delaying its sailing for 48 hours because of 'urgent repairs'. That would give you the chance to make your way to the port and get on to that ship. The other way would be for you to wave your pistols at the refuelling crew and demand to be refuelled, then take off and fly to Sweden."

We had our qualms about ever surviving flying into the gun barrels of the *Tirpitz* and all the other defences, but things were getting beyond a joke with ideas like walking off a Russian airfield, and asking non-English speaking Russians the way to their naval port. Then, getting permission to go into the port, because 'there's a ship waiting for us there'. We also wondered what sort of reaction there would be at an RAF airfield if a bunch of pistol-waiving Russian aircrew arrived, demanding fuel. Didn't "they" understand that threatening to shoot the refuelling crew could be seen by the Russians as a threatening act, which would probably mean being shot after incarceration in a Siberian camp?

An attack on the *Tirpitz* in Narvik or Altenfjord flying from – and returning to – Vaenga would have been well within the aircraft's range. Moscow would have to authorise the use of that base for the attack and to undertake to provide their low-grade fuel for the return flight to Sumburgh. That would mean revealing to the local Russian commanders details of the mission; security in that region was known to be lax, and the Murmansk area was a hotbed of spies. There was, therefore, a real risk that the Germans would become aware not just of the impending attack, but of how the attack may be launched. That could negate at a stroke all the determination and skill of the aircrews, and could result in a costly, abysmal failure. There was also the risk that the Russians might simply commandeer the aircraft and weapons for their own use. In those circumstances there would be no guarantee that the Russians would return, by any route, any of the 618 Squadron aircrew.

This may seem to have over-dramatised the relationship at operating level between the Russians and the Allies, but nearly 40 years after this period the British Ministry of Defence began an exhaustive enquiry after being given a list of more than 130 British servicemen that had allegedly been held in Soviet concentration camps after being freed by the Russians from German prisoner-of-war camps. In August 1992, after the break up of the former Union of Soviet Socialist Republics, the former Soviet Defence Ministry uncovered documents showing that more than 1,400 British servicemen died in the Soviet gulags. They included aircrew who were seen by the Russians to be useful for their knowledge and expertise.

We aircrew at Skitten could not contribute much in the way of ideas to overcome this problem of distance, other than to carry out precise fuel consumption tests. We spent a lot of time studying the 1:100,000 maps and the models of the anchorages at Kaa and Lang Fjords, not just to become completely familiar with the nature of the terrain but to work out how to cut valuable seconds from the time of the attack and escape. The extra consumption during the attack was so critical to the fuel that would be left to make an escape to Murmansk, Vaenga or into Sweden.

Norman Bottomley wrote to Jack Slessor at Coastal Command on 14th April 1943, in which he noted:–

"I think you would agree that the chances of a successful attack would be most seriously reduced if the position of the ships was unknown immediately before the operation was launched. The margin of operational range is so narrow and the hazards of search are so great that it is most desirable that the exact position of the ships should be known before the attack is launched." He made reference to a Most Secret note that he had had prepared dated 13th April. It says:–

"The Admiralty inform me that they are not certain of the present whereabouts of the German naval units situated in North Norway. They have been unable to obtain cover of this area for a period of three weeks and are therefore not confident that the ships are still on their original berths." The author concludes: "It will be seen that the possibilities of the German major naval units being in suitable positions for attack are problematical owing to the large number of berths that they can occupy. It would therefore be imperative before the projected operation that photographic reconnaissance cover is obtained, confirming their positions. Owing to the extreme distance of these targets, the obtaining of this cover is likely to prove difficult. . . The obtaining of information for attack is liable to considerably delay the date of any *Highball* operations if the weather turns unfavourable for PR cover".[2]

Whether the attack was to take place in Kaa (Altenfjord) or Bogen (Narvik), it was vital that the formation was on track as it came onto the coast, and so within range of the German Radio Direction Finding (RDF). The formation would accelerate to top speed at sea level, and the aircrew should concentrate on positioning to an agreed attack plan, and not have to waste time, fuel and attack formation while the planned path was being sought. So the critical items on the outward leg were a) maintaining the track, and b) turning at the right moment from that track onto the Norwegian coast.

The navigators were brought into discussions with Command Navigation Officers and Signals specialists, in formulating plans to increase the resources.

After setting course from Shetland, the navigators would be out of sight of land until seconds before the attack commenced. Each of them would be using the Course Setting Bomb Sight and the hand-held bearing compass to measure the wind direction, and to use their expertise in watching the spume or foam behind the wave tops to measure the force of the wind. He would then update his navigation plot, and tell his pilot the course that he calculated the formation should be steering. The heaviest burden rested on the navigator of the leading aircraft, but if he made an error, one of the other navigators could point this out on the Aldis lamp. Radio silence would be maintained after setting course.

Even the most competent navigators would be hard put to make a pinpoint landfall on an unfamiliar coastline after more than 900 miles of flying out of sight of land. If a major alteration of course had to be made, the formation would have to come up above 30 feet and so give away their approach to the German RDF and defenders. It would also use up valuable fuel. HQCC suggested that an experienced Norwegian crew, flying in a separate aircraft, could be assigned to lead the formation onto the target area.

A new navigation aid, known as GEE, had just come into service

[2]PRO AIR 15-442

but the demand for sets for mounting in aircraft far exceeded the production rate. The GEE system consisted of a cathode ray tube (CRT) in the aircraft receiving transmissions from three ground stations situated on a base line approximately 200 miles long. One transmitter was the Master "A", the others Slaves "B" and "C". The difference in time taken for the signals to reach the aircraft were measured on the CRT, and converted to position lines on a special GEE chart, to obtain a fix. The accuracy of the fix depended on the skill of the navigator using the CRT, the range and height of the aircraft from the transmitters and whether the GEE grid intersected acutely or obtusely. The transmissions from the nearest GEE stations gave position lines at acute angles, with diminished accuracy. At 1,000 feet the aircraft might have been able to pick up signals at 200 to 250 miles from the chain, but at sea level the range would be so limited as to be of no practical use.

After discussion at various levels – on the squadron, and at Coastal Command Headquarters, – the C-in-C asked that two Royal Navy submarines be made available to mark the track on the outward leg. Each submarine would be positioned at a predetermined point along the track, and at appointed times, would transmit homing signals for the briefest possible times. The navigators would use these transmissions to check and adjust the course being flown.

The aircraft would use back bearings on Sumburgh at the start of the run. The first submarine should be positioned at approximately 66°N 07°30'E; the aircraft would receive bearings both before and for 30 minutes after passing over the submarine. The furthest of the two submarines would be positioned in the area 71°N 18°E and would also act as a marker of the turning point to the coast. The use of the two submarines as navigation aids would help ensure that the formation was able to stay out of range of the RDF operators on Lofoten Islands. The transmissions from the surfaced submarines would have to be few and very brief, to protect themselves. The Navy could also lay on some suitable "spoof" radio traffic. The Chiefs of Staff Committee meeting on 17th May, told of this request, was also informed that the Navy had been asked to make a submarine available immediately for training in homing by the aircrews.

The Signals specialist suggested fitting Medium Frequency Direction Finding MF/DF loops onto the Mosquitos. The navigator would then rotate that loop until he picked up the maximum signal strength from a known transmitter; an azimuth scale below the rotating pole would show the bearing of that signal source. To obtain a fix, more than one bearing, from different transmitters, is needed. The most accurate fix derives from widely spaced transmitters. In our case, the transmitters were relatively close, so that the lines of the bearings would make a long, narrow triangle – and a poor fix. Hutch decided that D/F loops would not be fitted.

The C-in-C had also indicated that a cruiser, or similar warship, should be located in the Kola Peninsular – a tract of land in North Russia on the west side of which is the port of Murmansk – which would transmit homing signals after the attack, to guide the Mossies to the Russian airfield at Vaenga.

The planners were assuming that the Russians would be given little or no warning of the attack on the *Tirpitz* in Altenfjord (or Kaa Fjord). The warship would have to find some acceptable pretext for remaining in port, and its commanding officer could hopefully persuade the Russians not to fire on the Mossies as they limped their way to Vaenga. The warship would be working its D/F on 385 Kcs and transmitting courses to steer to 618 Squadron aircrew on 6000Kcs. An RAF Flying Control Officer would have to be on board to provide such approach assistance as was possible.

The warship would also be carrying a supply of drop-tanks, and a small RAF maintenance crew who would hurriedly ready the flyable Mossies for the return leg to Sumburgh. Replacement flying clothing would also have to be available.

Furthermore, the transmitting station at Rugby should work out, as a matter of urgency, the signals organisation to be used in connection with the submarines and with surface naval craft that would have to be on the route homewards when – eventually – the surviving aircraft were flown back to Britain.

The time of day at which the attack should be carried out was also important. At the latitude of Altenfjord, in late May, the sun is above the horizon all day. The best approach to the target was out of the sun, and because that approach would be from the west, the most appropriate time for the attack would be 17.17 hours GMT. At that time the sun would bear 290° from the target on 26th May, and some 6 minutes later the following month.

The lack of up-to-date intelligence on the exact whereabouts of the *Tirpitz*, and of the size of the naval force that was protecting it, had to be overcome before final detailed briefings could be embarked on. The position of the sun, and the length of shadows cast from the high steep slopes of the fjord, would determine the best time of day for the succession of reconnaissance flights which would have to be laid on. It was not unreasonable to assume that cloud would prevent ac-ccurate reconnaissance on at least half the flights.

The Mossie crews would transfer from Skitten or Turnberry to Sumburgh and then would be put on stand-by for days, waiting for the interpretation of reconnaissance flights and for the right weather forecast.

Meanwhile, the state of suspense continued. Some of the aircrew were able to grab a few days' leave, with that awful journey on the Jellicoe leave train. But, the initial date for mounting the op. had passed, and the absence of a defined new date was yet another torture implement. A pilot was only able to make further proving runs after the modifications to the stores and the release gear. But pilots and navigators alike could not avoid being continually immersed in the problems of the tactics of the attack and escape.

The Chiefs of Staff Committee were told that the Russians had been supplied with details and drawings of the Upkeep weapon after the raid by 617 Squadron on the Ruhr dams on the night of 16/17th May 1943.

The regular meeting of the Chiefs of Staff Committee monitoring the *Highball* project were informed on 13th June that, if the technical problems with the stores could be resolved, 618 Squadron would be operationally fit by the end of June. (At the time of that report, the squadron had six fully modified Mosquitos in service.) The C-in-C, Coastal was working on the possibility of mounting the attack on "an objective in Northern waters" by 12th July, but a change of target to the Italian ships would extend that date.

By the 27th June 1943, the problems of the endurance of the Mosquito aircraft were starting to emerge, as is shown in the report of the regular Chiefs of Staff Committee:–

"As a result of further investigation by Coastal Command into the planning of Operation *Servant*, it has been established that, contrary to the previous expectations, the range of the Mosquito fitted with

German battlecruiser Tirpitz *shortly after commissioning.* (WZ-Bilddienst)

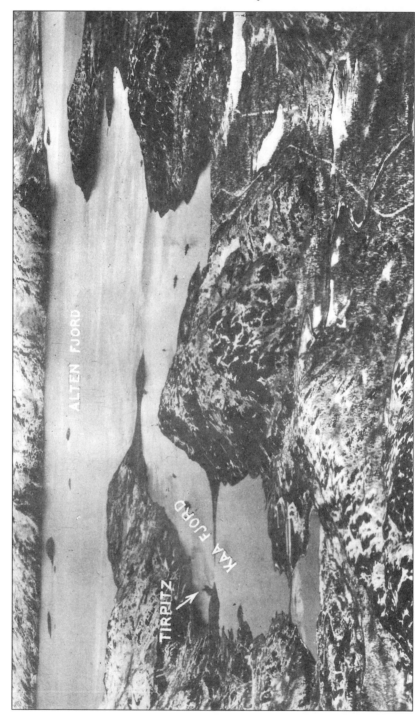

Photo reconnaissance view of Kaa and Alten Fjords in March 1943. Tirpitz is lying off its normal anchorage. (Imperial War Museum)

P.R. close-up of Tirpitz *in April 1943 on its normal anchorage, in shelter of steep pine-covered hills. (*Imperial War Museum*)*

Another view of Tirpitz with service vessels alongside, affording added protection from possible Highball attack, April 1943. (Imperial War Museum)

drop tanks is insufficient to undertake attacks on objectives in Altenfjord from bases in the UK. It is now considered by the C-in-C that, due to tactical factors, the onward flight from target to Vaenga would have to be done at maximum speed and at ground level. This would so increase consumption as to exhaust the fuel carried, leaving no allowance whatever for operational factors. Even if the attacks were delivered on objectives at Narvik, there would be insufficient margin of fuel to allow aircraft to reach Vaenga. It is therefore considered impractical to undertake attacks on enemy ships in Narvik or Altenfjord from bases in the UK, unless deliberate abandonment of aircraft over Sweden were contemplated.

"Attacks on objectives in Trondheim are however possible from bases in the UK. If the enemy capital ships are found to be in Narvik or Altenfjord, the only practical method of attacking with any reasonable chance of reaching base after that attack is to operate from and return to a base in North Russia.

"The C-in-C, Coastal Command has suggested that the operation could best be carried out from Vaenga. It is clear, therefore, that if we are to count on the possibility of attacking the enemy ships in Narvik or Altenfjord, we must make preparations for the operation of 618 Squadron at Vaenga. This will include the the transportation by sea of certain key personnel and equipment well in advance of the date of the operation. It would also necessitate our communicating to the Russians our intention and obtaining the necessary sanction for the operation. The Russians have no knowledge of *Highball*, and it may prove necessary to give them some indication of the special weapon and secrecy would thereby be prejudiced.

"There is also the risk that aircraft en route to Russia may be compelled to land in enemy occupied territory and thereby prejudice security. The project, however, offers the following advantages:–

1. the navigation would be greatly simplified,

2. the objectives would be within comparatively easy range of base, and the aircraft would have ample fuel to meet the needs of any emergency,

3. the approach to the target could be made from an unexpected direction, possibly without RDF warning and with complete surprise,

4. the operation could be more safely timed as a result of more up-to-date PR,

5. the met. problems would be greatly eased and opportunities of good weather far more readily seized.

"It is therefore recommended by the committee that a decision be made to postpone the date of the operation by one month, that is until about the 12th August, by which time, subject to clearance of present technical difficulties, adequate preparatory arrangements can be made in order that the squadron can operate from a suitable base in North Russia. Also that negotiations be opened with the Russian authorities immediately with a view to obtaining sanction to use the air base at Vaenga for this purpose and for providing all the necessary facilities in North Russia.

"The C-in-C, Coastal has been requested to examine the question of increasing the size of 618 Squadron and making recommendations as to the number of crews that should be provided in the unit initially to meet the requirements laid down by the Chiefs of Staff to be ready for attacks either in the North or in the Mediterranean. A decision has not yet been made on this."

The remainder of this paper discusses the numbers of aircraft and the current state of development of the weapon and bomb sight.

Hutch, as Commanding Officer, may have been kept in the picture as regards both the intention to make preparations for an attack on Italian capital ships and of the firm recommendation to use Vaenga for the attack on *Tirpitz*.

The aircrews had only an inkling of the debate that was going on at high level, and were left to carry on the training/study routine – always with the feeling that, when the Big Day comes, few would be likely to survive all the hazards that had to be overcome.

618 Squadron was, apparently, off to North Russia. *But nobody told the aircrew!*

Spirits amongst the aircrew might have been raised had they been aware of this recommendation to move the base for the operation from Sumburgh to Vaenga. Each pilot and navigator conjured up his own vision of what those minutes and seconds of the attack would be like – once the "Attack, attack" order had been given. The tiredness and strain of flying low over the North Sea, and keeping eyes open for the first dots on the horizon that could rapidly enlarge into enemy fighters – all that would quickly give way to a new alertness, an increase in the heartbeat rate as the adrenalin began pumping, and a mixture of fear and elation with the realisation that The Big Event was just about to begin. The vision would follow these lines:–

"No time for a last minute fag – too late for the last minute pee – didn't want one five minutes ago, but it'll take too long to get Percy out from all the harness, Mae West straps and clothing.

"Pilots – check the bomb sight, check fuel tank levels, throttles ready to be opened to full 3,000 rpm with boost at +14 lb.sq.in. Navigators – tell the pilot the course to steer after the attack, just in case the navigator gets killed or knocked out, put the small chart board into the nav. bag, pick up the hand held camera and check that all switches are on and the lens is clean.

"If Francis French has done a good job as the leading navigator, and we make a spot-on landfall, Jerry's RDF operators will have to get a move on to get the warning message through to the gunners and defenders on the shore and on the ships. Even as we each open up to full throttle and start racing over the islands at the entrance to Altenfjord, the sirens will be sounding and men will be rushing to man the flak guns and to start up the smoke pots.

"Don't know whether it would be best if there was complete cloud cover. It would give us cover from fighters on the way out, but that could mean we'd be flying amongst stuffed clouds (where the cloud base is lower than the tops of the surrounding hills). But it would also mean that the target's going to be less easy to find, as the water, the ships and the sky will all be shades of grey.

"We'll be coming in from the west, making our run in right on the deck with taps fully opened. The shore batteries and anti-aircraft guns will open up from either side of Altenfjord. Probably, the coastal batteries will be trained in the art of splash-shelling. At nought feet, that can do more damage than trying for a direct hit, and as we'll be in formation, there won't be any room for manouevre.

"Once we're in Altenfjord we've got to be ready for a turn to starboard, turning in to Kaafjord. We'll have to stay in a gentle turn, going through about 120 degrees, before lining up for the final run onto the target."

"Our model shows that there'll be a spit of land on our starboard as we come abreast of the entrance to Kaafjord, and those latest photos taken on 1st June by a PR aircraft show that the battleship *Lutzow* is at anchor on the other side of that spit. So she'll be the first

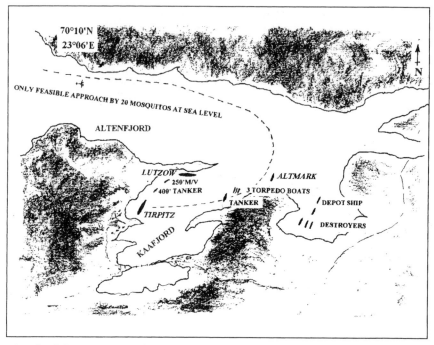

Sketch of shipping in Kaafjord, based on a PR sortie on 1st June, 1943

ship to join the shore batteries in opening up – and she'll have us in full view from the word 'Go' until the lucky survivors make their getaway.

"There hasn't been much discussion in the briefing room on the detailed plan of attack. The length of the *Tirpitz* is about 830 feet. To cut down the chances of lateral misses, the stores will have to be aimed at the central section – that'll be about 550 feet of the target width. The wing span of a Mossie is over 50 feet, so the largest number of aircraft that could make a line abreast attack – without serious risk of collision – would be four. So we'd have to be going in in five waves of four aircraft, releasing 8 stores in each wave.

"The *Tirpitz* has 110 anti-aircraft guns – imagine that!! – and she'll be able to open fire with a near horizontal barrage, with practically no deflection and over a very small angle. We'll be in sight just as we start the right wheel. Add to that the fire power of the *Lutzow*, throw in for good measure the smaller guns on the destroyers and torpedo boats and whatever the shore batteries are going to be throwing, and there's not a cat in hell's chance of flying straight and level through that and coming out the other side in one piece."

"We'll have to tighten the turn for the final run-in – to keep away from the rocky promontory that is opposite the target. Can't have the port wingmen in a gentle·climb and dive over the land while the other 3 Mossies are straight and level. The stores from the wingmen could bounce erratically and bring someone else down.

"The time interval between each wave will have to be the absolute minimum – to try and save the lives of the poor sods in the rear waves. By the time they come in, the smoke pots will be starting to obscure the target, and the gunners will have got the ranges by then. The stores from, say, the first wave will take a few seconds to bounce to the *Tirpitz* and another couple of seconds to sink to depth charge level. The stores have to be released while flying straight and level, because, if not, the gyroscopic effect to keep them upright will be skewed, and they'll be erratic. But the stores won't have delayed action fuses, so the Mossies in the second and later waves may have to fly through debris from the explosions. Then the outside pair might be lucky enough to do a tight turn below the decks of the ship, but the poor sods in the right hand Mossie will come bang on to the *Lutzow*.

"Of course, all that assumes that the smoke and flak bursts haven't obscured the other ships and the hillsides. So if the *Tirpitz* somehow misses us, we've a good chance of crashing into something in the smoke."

"Then if there are bits of us left – if the pilot's injuries are slight enough for him to fly, and if the Mossie is able to pull us over the mountains – where are we making for? Shell shocked, beaten up, and desperately short of fuel, are we then going to have to find a friendly aircraft carrier somewhere out to the west, then bale out into the sea inside the Arctic Circle? Are we going to head for the pine forests and come crashing down in some isolated place where no-one would even hear us going in? Are we going to hope to find some marshy tundra on which to do a belly landing? We've survived so far – now it's a question of which way to die. Bloody hell! Who wants a VC anyway?"

There cannot have been a man on 618 who wasn't thinking along those lines. What made this seemingly suicidal operation more difficult to cope with was the way the initial urgency had degenerated into slow motion but with life-threatening imponderables still unresolved, and the complete inability to talk to anyone – particularly one's loved ones – about any part of it.

A 618 Squadron Mosquito releasing inert Highballs *against a target warship in Loch Striven.* (Brooklands Museum)

ABOVE: *Two stores, the first released (left) about to overtake the second one, released 3 seconds later.* BELOW: *A civilian and a Service observer scurrying for cover on deck of HMS* Malaya *as an inert store pierces the hull above the water line.* (Brooklands Museum)

ABOVE: *The hole in HMS* Malaya.
BELOW: *A formation of inert stores off RAF Skitten.*
(Brooklands Museum)

CHAPTER 7

Everything Changes

During May and June, the aircrews were mostly employed in ferrying the aircraft. Continued practise at low level flying over the sea was non-productive, as this did not require too much skill as a training exercise devoid of the tension of flying into hostile waters and the impending attack. There had not been any opportunity for the full squadron to fly off for a mock attack, as there was not a time when the squadron was at full strength on one airfield. Boredom was starting to set in, but with the nagging thought ever present in the background that when the op. does take place it will be a one-way trip.

Boredom showed itself in several ways. The Beaufighters which had been lent for training were lying at Skitten awaiting removal by the ATA to a maintenance airfield, as they were barely airworthy. On 26th June we had acquired from RAF Leuchars a de Havilland Dominie, X7383, a delightful 6 seater biplane with fabric-covered fuselage and wings, to be used as a communications aircraft. RAF Turnberry was a training airfield, with 618 Squadron perched at its most remote edge. One afternoon, discussion started in the flight hut on whether the Mosquito or the Dominie was the fastest to get off the ground. There was only one way to settle the argument – that was to put it to the test. Emjay Melville-Jackson would take the Dominie and Doug Turner the Mosquito.

Chiefy was called in to get both aircraft ready. Bets were laid; the winner would be the aircraft that got its wheels off the ground for the last time, no bouncing being permitted. Chiefy gave the word that both aircraft were ready, and on the "Ready, Steady, Go" the two pilots leapt from their seats and out to the aircraft. Nobody had laid down any rules about proper taxying, or telling Flying Control that something unusual was about to take place. Seconds later, the two aircraft turned into wind, opened throttles and charged across the runways and the grass. The Dominie made it first by a narrow margin.

They turned into the circuit and the Dominie gracefully followed the Mosquito in landing perfectly on the runway in use, and they joyfully parked. It was a pity that they hadn't checked with the tower, because a very irate controller summoned both pilots to the tower, where they came face to face with an Air Commodore from Training Command who happened to be getting clearance before leaving in his Proctor. Not only did they get balled out there and then, but Hutch got it in the neck from the Air Officer Admin at HQCC. The Dominie was, however, returned to Leuchars on 17th August, still in one piece.

At Skitten, on a clear afternoon on 20th June, a Mosquito was seen to climb over the airfield to about 9,000 feet, then from a dive to about 2,500 feet, it pulled up into a power climb, culminating in a loop. It completed the aerobatic by pulling out at about 1,000 feet, at around 400 mph, before losing speed. Hutch happened to be looking out of his office window so he missed nothing. Doug Turner and Des Curtis were marched in by the Adjutant, and had to endure a withering blast from Hutch, who quite rightly didn't want to lose an aircraft, or even a crew, through such antics. He was a very sensitive man, despite his burly appearance, and was conscious of the ennui that was becoming apparent amongst his men.

On 17th June, DZ555 was flying on a consumption test, in the course of which it passed across Holy Island, off the Northumberland coast. It was suddenly fired on and hit, causing the pilot to make a one-wheel landing back at Turnberry.

On 1st July 1943 Hutch received orders from HQCC that the unit at Turnberry was to close, and the squadron would withdraw back to Skitten.

With most of the squadron back at their base at Skitten, the level of activity up at flights was a lot less, and the number of hours flown by each of the crews was small. There was no sign that the German High Command was about to move the *Tirpitz* from its lair in Altenfjord to a port that was more easily accessible to Mosquitos. So the main topic of conversation amongst the crews was still – where they would be coming to earth or to sea after the attack. The pessimistic johnnies said that it was not a question of "if you're going to die" but "how".

There was still no mention at the regular briefing sessions of the decision to move 618 Squadron to Vaenga. Maybe Hutch had privately come to the conclusion that that was a pretty remote possibility and thought it best not to add further confusion. If so, he was right – because the idea never materialised.

The trials against the *Courbet* were not being wholly successful, and they were then postponed while the boffins worked on problems that were showing up with the release gear in the bomb bay, and with the regular running of the stores over calm water.

The trials moved once more to Manston and the nearby range; in early July there was a prospect that the problems with the aircraft had been resolved.

There were a sizeable number of stores filled with HE lying in a secure hangar on Sumburgh airfield, should the order be given to mount Operation *Servant*. Yet modifications were still being made to the stores that were being used in the trials. For example, some stores were experimentally clad in an outer jacket of ash wood. Designs and specifications were being drawn up for an outer casing of heavier gauge metal, using no wood. But the manufacturers had made it clear that, even if the highest priorities were accorded to providing the materials and the presses, a full month would be required to start production. Those manufacturers must have been going round the bend, trying to get on with completing the production order.

The high powered committee, in its report to the Chiefs of Staff Committee of 12th July, reflected continuing faith in the satisfactory development of the *Highball* weapon, and believed there was reason to hope that the squadron might be in operation about the middle of September.

There was concern at all levels from the Chief of Air Staff and the C-in-C Coastal Command to the Commanding Officer of 618 Squadron of the effect of the delays and uncertainty on the aircrew. Pilots and navigators had been rushed from operational squadrons to create this squadron, and had clearly understood and accepted that the attack on the *Tirpitz* would involve very heavy losses. The fact that the operational planning had stalled did not take away the continual nagging thought in the mind of each pilot and navigator that one day soon he was probably going to die. It was highly undesirable that they should be kept hanging around, doing 40 minute flights in the vicinity of the airfield with the occasional navigation exercise.

It was possible that one or two senior people who had been so vocal a few months earlier in advocating that 30 Mossies should be modified and that inert and HE-filled bombs should be produced were now getting panicky. What if Winston Churchill should ask why a whole squadron of Mosquitos and experienced crews were not in the front line of battle, or why bomb making capacity had been diverted away from bombs that could be dropped immediately on German economic or military targets? Whose heads would be rolling?

The need to remove the threat posed by the *Tirpitz* and the immense propaganda value of doing so continued to occupy minds in both the RAF and the RN.

On 2nd July 1943, Air Vice Marshal Norman Bottomley ACAS (Ops) and Admiral E. J. P. Brind, ACNS (H) submitted a report to the First Sea Lord and the Chief of the Air Staff, putting up the proposition that the Royal Navy should be authorised to mount an attack using 6 "X" Class midget submarines. That project was codenamed Operation *Source,* and the authors noted that such an operation could be ready for mounting in the second half of September. Norman Bottomley was, of course, fully acquainted with all aspects of Operation *Servant* and the *Highball* stores.

Bottomley and Brind recommended that Operation *Source* should be mounted at the best time irrespective of Operation *Servant* or any other air operation at present envisaged; and that Operation *Servant* should not be mounted against the *Tirpitz.* The Chiefs of Staff gave the go-ahead to Operation *Source,* and the raid by three Royal Navy midget submarines was carried out against the battleship in Altenfjord on 22nd September 1943. (In that gallant action, Sub. X5 was lost with all hands outside the inner protective net. Subs. X6 and X7 laid their charges beneath the *Tirpitz,* after overcoming great difficulties. Two crewmen were drowned, the remainder taken prisoner. Both commanders, Cameron and Place, DSC, were awarded the Victoria Cross.)

The decision to mount Operation *Source* served to highlight the problem of what to do with 618 Squadron and its *Highball* version of the bouncing bomb.

The effort to defeat the U-boats was as important as ever, so the best solution would be to use the *Highball* stores in the attack against the U-boats. The pre-selected depth charge pistols in the HE-filled stores at Sumburgh had been set to 36 feet, whereas the draught of a surfaced U-boat was only 16 feet. The vertical profile of a U-boat was flask-shaped, in marked contrast to that of the *Tirpitz*. So the unique feature of the backward spinning store – the ability to cling to the vertical surface of its target until reaching depth charge level – would be lost.

Sir Charles Portal, Chief of Air Staff, wrote to the First Sea Lord, on 23rd July 1943, advising him of the proposal to use *Highball* in anti-submarine work. MAP had recommended that the outer casing of the store would be removed, so creating a cylindrical shape not unlike that used against the Ruhr dams, and that they should be given forward spin. The removal of the outer casing would disguise the spinning movement, and so would not prejudice security for the future use of *Highball* against capital ships. By making it spin forwards, the store would not run on the surface, and would thus rapidly sink to depth charge level.

When he was brought into the discussions on the employment of 618 Squadron on anti-submarine work, Norman Bottomley made the extraordinary observation that "any operation with *Highball* is likely to require a high standard of navigation and that it may be necessary for the crews to land and take off by night". That was truly a statement of the obvious! It might have been more relevant to say that the Mosquitos would be joining the hundreds of other aircraft – Sunderlands, Catalinas, Fortresses, Hudsons, Liberators, Wellingtons etc – which were combing the high seas and enemy coastal waters day and night for U-boats. These Mosquitos would not be carrying ASV, and so would be limited to making visual searches of the assigned patrol areas.

Hutch briefed the crews on the new role, for which training would begin at once. Flg Off F. J. Rose, the Armaments Officer, would supervise the reversal of the motor leads in the bomb bays to give forward spin. The first task would be to bring from Sumburgh a sufficient number of HE-filled stores to get operations under way, and Flg Off Rose would get the armourers to strip off the casings. Flying programmes would include practise drops of inert stores, spinning forwards, from a height of 150 feet, and a minimum airspeed of 220 knots, with 120 feet spacing between the stores on impact. Initially, the stores would be released while the Mossie was approaching

Sinclair Bay, so that the drop could be watched by Jim Rogerson, the
Vickers Representative; it would also offer the possibility that some
of the stores might be recovered.

The aircrew were glad to have an immediate sense of purpose –
a new challenge, to which they readily responded. There was one
anxious moment when Flg Off Doug Turner, making a run with two
HE stores, suffered a hang up. Neither of the stores would separate
from the Mossie, in spite of every attempt to jolt them free. Flying
Control made urgent contact with Flg Off Rose, who calmly said that
Turner should land and taxi to the remotest grass parking on the
airfield. Rose would join him there. Doug Turner made one of his
better landings, and, given half a chance, he and the author would
have leapt from the Mossie as soon as he'd switched off the magnetos. But as the side hatch opened, Rose poked his head up and said,
"When I give the thumbs up, and not before, give the tit a press". He
disappeared back down the underbelly, and we sat in sweaty silence.
A short while later, Rose walked away, then at about thirty yards,
turned and gave the Thumbs Up sign. Doug pressed the tit, and we
felt the thuds as the two stores dropped to the grass below us.

Each crew made a number of runs with HE stores out in the open
sea. With no distracting flak from the target, it was easy to make
a near-perfect drop each time. On just about every run, the crews
reported that the stores, instead of immediately disappearing below
the surface, would catch a wave top, and bounce in the most erratic
way. So much obviously depended on which part of the cylinder
struck the most resistant part of the wave. There was a real danger of
the store bouncing into the path of the Mossie. It could, just as easily,
bounce over the top of the low superstructure of the surfaced U-boat,
giving the crew a grandstand view of this secret weapon.

The idea was born on 23rd July and died on 7th September.

Back in the briefing room, Hutch started to talk about some
strange tunnel entrances that low-level PRU Spitfires had photo-
graphed in the Pas de Calais area. Some of them had rail tracks
leading from them. He confided that there was reason to believe that
the Germans were intending to bring into use a new rocket type
weapon, which would be fired from these tunnels. He had been asked
for his opinion on whether we could "roll" our stores into these
tunnels. It was, of course, just as practicable to carry out pin-point

bombing with the *Highball* stores as with conventional HE, and vice versa. Nothing more was heard of this scheme, but of course the Germans did bring into use in mid-1944 the V1 "doodlebug" and the V2 rocket.

Lord Louis Mountbatten, the Chief of Combined Operations sought the approval of the Chiefs of Staff on 30th July for trials of both *Upkeep* and *Highball* against walls that represented the anti-tank walls on the north coast of France. His request was met with a lukewarm response, saying that 6 stores loaded into 3 Mosquitos would be needed on each breach. There was a heavy demand for Mosquitos elsewhere. The Chiefs of Staff suggested that RP's (Rocket projectiles) fired from ramp-carrying tanks may be more effective.

Each of the tasks that were assigned to the squadron seemed doomed to failure – no part of which could be laid at the feet of the the squadron personnel.

Days became longer, as the workload decreased. Volleyball teams were getting up to championship standard, and soccer and rugby games against other Services teams in the area were fixed up.

On 22 August 1943, an important announcement appeared in Squadron Daily Routine Orders:–

"Dancing classes will begin in the Station gym, under the instruction of LAC Sixsmith, from 19.00 hours for three hours. LAC Sixsmith is willing to continue classes if these are supported. A squadron dance will be held in the gym on 25th August."

The rot had set in – there was nothing else to stimulate the mind or body! The squadron dance turned out to be the farewell party.

On 28th August, two Mosquitos were authorised to make surprise low-level dummy attacks on RAF Peterhead. A clipped-wing Spitfire squadron stationed there had seen little activity of late, and these attacks would test their state of readiness to scramble. The Mossie flown by Keith Ellis and Ron Dodd cut things a bit fine by shaving off a wing tip on the top of a church spire. They made a forced landing in a field, and both spent a while in hospital suffering from burns. Doug Turner and the author, in DZ545, made several passes and were intercepted by a Spitfire. In the chase over the fields that followed, the Spitfire must have been caught in the turbulence of the Mosquito slipstream. It flipped over and crashed. Those exercises were, quite properly, discontinued.

The committee that was working under the Chiefs of Staff reported on 7th September that the Commander-in-Chief, Coastal Command had decided to disperse the majority of personnel on 618 Squadron until technical trials were finally completed and a decision taken to employ the squadron in its original role. A nucleus of skilled personnel would continue with such operational trials as were necessary and to help in developing the techniques asssociated with using *Highball* in its proper role. The Chiefs of Staff concurred with this decision.

On 11th September the squadron was grounded at Skitten; flying trials were to continue from Wick and Turnberry.

By the 18th October, most of the aircrew had delivered Mossies to maintenance units, and gone on their way. The squadron was reduced to a cadre of the C.O., 4 aircrew and an appropriate proportion of ground staff. At the year-end, squadron strength at Wick was 29 officers, 24 senior NCO's, 112 corporals and airmen, and 17 WAAF. 8618 Servicing Echelon comprised 75 NCO's and airmen.

The cadre of aircrew continued the research work with Barnes Wallis and his team. Welded skin stores, when released against the *Courbet* in September, had deviated and missed the recovery nets. They had still not been recovered a month later. But in November and December, Sqn Ldr Melville-Jackson, and Flt Lts Stephen and Hopwood released a total of 25 stores against the *Courbet*.

At Porton, trials were carried out against a hard concrete wall in an endeavour to establish if the weapon had any potential as a land weapon.

Hutch and his team flew to Valley in Anglesey, from where they made several sorties to determine the feasibility of putting *Highball* into a tunnel, to establish whether a wood-covered store with steel plates would stand the impact, and to test the efficiency of the self-destruct fuse. The tunnel selected was a disused Great Western Railway single track tunnel 100 yards long near Maenclochog, Pembroke. 12 drops were made from 50 to 100 feet, 10 at 200 mph and 2 at 300 mph, all with forward spin at 900 rpm.

Two of the stores went straight through the tunnel, and 7 hit the face of the tunnel. The crews reckoned that double track tunnel with its wider entrance offered the prospect of a 75% success rate. When the structure of the tunnel, mostly brickwork, was examined following explosion of some stores, the results were disappointingly small. It was accepted that it was not worth maintaining a squadron especially for this purpose.[1]

A special report dated October 1943 to the Chiefs of Staff recalled that originally there were to be 2 squadrons requiring 60 modified Mosquitos. But now, there were no heavy enemy units in the Mediterranean, and the *Tirpitz* had been seriously damaged by the midget submarines. The remaining enemy heavy units were outside the effective range of *Highball* Mosquitos.

"The redesigned *Highball* gives great promise but no proof of its technical satisfaction versus capital ships in harbour. It is not yet possible to do rough water trials so we cannot say how effective the weapon would be versus merchant or naval ships at sea. Also, if they were so used, they would forfeit the element of surprise if greater prize targets were offered. The effective use versus Japanese capital ships would depend on the element of surprise, which would be lost if *Highball* was used on the Dutch or Norwegian coasts in anti-shipping." That committee recommended that all but 30 aircraft should be re-converted for normal bombing use.[2]

On 8th January 1944, Wg Cdr Hutchinson and Flg Off French were taking off in DZ353 at Vickers Armstrong, Weybridge, when both undercarriage legs collapsed. Fortunately neither of them suffered serious injury. This was their second accident during take-off at Weybridge. It is possible that even an experienced pilot like Hutch had been correcting too harshly the tendency of the Mossie to turn to port. If too much engine or braking was applied, a zig-zag path along the runway developed; that in turn caused the centre of gravity to try and travel in a different direction to the main wheels. This so increased the sideways load on the oleo legs that one or both would collapse.

In a separate incident, John Walker and Leon Murray flew from Wick to Hatfield on 10th June 1944. Unfortunately the landing T had been wrongly positioned, causing them to come in downwind on the grass. Having difficulty in coming to a stop, and seeing a concrete air

[1] PRO AIR 20-1000
[2] PRO AIR 20-1000

raid shelter approaching just ahead, John Walker managed a ground loop; the undercarriage collapsed. The ambulance took the crew, shaken but otherwise unhurt, to the control tower, where they were quickly joined by Sir Geoffrey de Havilland, who had watched the scene from his garden.

Reverting to the dispersal of some of the aircrew, on 8th September, Flg Off A. T. Wickham, Plt Off WED Makins, Flt Lt A. S. Cussens and Flt Sgt A. W. Munro were posted to RAF Sculthorpe, and so returned to Bomber Command. (Tony Wickham was the pilot of the PR Mosquito that played an important part in assessing the success of the raid on Amiens prison on 18th February 1944, by Mosquitos of 464, 487 and 21 Squadrons. That raid was one of the great achievements in military aviation history.) Others were posted to RAF Benson to join PR squadrons, or were returned to the Coastal Command ship-busting Beaufighter squadrons. We come back to them later in this story.

CHAPTER 8

The New Theatre

On 7th May 1944, the War Cabinet Chiefs of Staff Committee received a report stating that the *Tirpitz* was no longer a profitable target for *Highball*.

At the end of October 1943 a signal had been sent by Air Ministry to the RAF Mission in Washington, telling them that it was hoped that the *Highball* trials would be successfully completed by the year end, and then seeking the United States reaction to the employment of 618 Squadron in the Pacific theatre. Air Ministry had identified that there was the potential for an attack on the Japanese fleet at Truk, using bases at Kavieng, Bouganville and Nadang, 600, 840 and 900 nautical miles respectively from the target. The expectation was that those bases would be in Allied hands by May 1944.

Of the Japanese fleet, half its strength was in battleships and carriers, which were likely to be using bases in the Singapore – Borneo – Phillipines area for some months. The United States operations could force the Japanese to withdraw back to Japan by November 1944.

The bases in that triangle would be well suited for attack by *Highball* aircraft, but owing to the distance from our nearest airfields – in the Cocos Islands – the operations would have to be carrier based. The nearest point to which carriers could approach the Japanese anchorages would be 360 miles, making it impossible to mount a 'land-to-carrier' or vice vera operation.

Cdr "Nine Lives" Brown, RN, an experienced test pilot, had made the first successful landing of a Mosquito on a carrier in January. It had been proven that a lightly loaded aircraft, fitted with an arrester hook during production, could use a fleet carrier. Trials were now urgently needed to determine the feasibility of using Mosquitos with operational all-up weights, with hooks fitted as a modification, and being flown by average Service pilots in reasonable weather conditions.

The Chiefs of Staff were told on 12th May that those trials indicated that 12 *Highball* Mosquitos could be carried on one fleet carrier.

Lord Portal, Chief of Air Staff, had decided that the task should be given to the RAF and not to the Fleet Air Arm.[1]

29 *Highball* Mosquito Mk IV's, of which 24 would be shipped to the Far East together with 3 PR Mosquito Mk XVI's, would be needed. The PR aircraft would fly the reconnaissance missions to locate, and keep under surveillance, potential targets. All aircraft would have to have an arrester hook fitted, calling for strengthening of the rear fuselage section; de Havillands needed 5 months to turn them out. The aircraft would be refitted with Merlin 25 engines for improved low-level speed. Other modifications were fitting windscreen wipers, armoured windscreens and twin brake drums. A new air turbine for spinning the stores, a new type of safety fuse, a 'bomb distributor', a radio altimeter and the Barnes Wallis bombsight would be fitted. The bomb distributor would be set to give a 0.3 second time gap between the release of each store. There would not be time to tropicalise them – a task that might later be carried out in the Far East.

The stores that would be taken, with the squadron, to the Far East would weigh 1,280 lbs, containing 600 lbs of Torpex. The space between the charge case and the spherical outer cover would be filled with aerated resin, to act as a shock absorber.

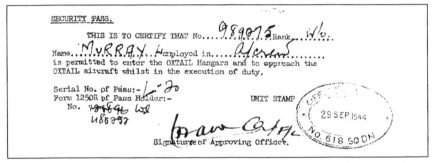

Special security pass issued to aircrew and servicing personnel of 618 Squadron.

618 Squadron would immediately be reconstituted in 18 Group at RAF Wick, from where it would move to Beccles in Norfolk, under 16 Group. The squadron would be referred to as a 'Special Minelaying Unit' under the codeword: *"Oxtail"*.

It was reckoned that 14 of the original crews were still available. 15 new crews would be posted in from operational squadrons, the task

[1] PRO AIR 20-2618

of selection being made easier this time, because some Coastal Command strike squadrons were by then equipped with Mosquito Mark VI F. 5 crews would come from PR squadrons. Most of the new crews were posted in w.e.f. 11th July 1944 (See Appendix ii). Others to join the squadron were Flt Lt J. S. Boyd, as Senior Medical Officer, Flg Off Payne as Signals Officer, Flg Off Bailey as Intelligence Officer. Flt Lt Smith came from Wick to Beccles as Engineer Officer.

RAF Beccles was unoccupied at the time. It was transferred to 16 Group, Coastal Command in August, and instructions given that no other units were to be permitted on the airfield. Work began immediately on marking out the runways, a) for dummy carrier landings and take-offs, and b) for practice bombing runs, for which the bow and stern of a ship were marked at one end, and intervals marked along the length of the runway.

Time had once again become of the essence. Top priority had to be given to getting the pilots trained in deck take-off and landing. The few Mosquitos that were available were rightly considered too precious to be used for this initial training; the planners considered that it was 'desirable but not essential' that training should include one or two take-offs and landings on carriers.

There was not a lot of clearance between the wing tip of a Mosquito and the superstructure of the large carriers then in service – and those were the days before sloping take-off ramps had been invented. The tendency to swing to port on take off was well-known. The width of the flight deck, and the pilot's concentration on the unfamiliar surroundings, could magnify the significance of that tendency. Capt Brown was made available for two days to train the pilots in deck landings, on the painted strip at Beccles. Lt. Keith, RN was sent on loan to Beccles as Deck Landing Officer; he in turn trained Flt Lt Goodman to be a 'batman'. (Flt Lt Goodman had served in India, from where he was repatriated sick; he was released from the squadron when it left the UK as he was barred from further service in the tropics.)

The Fleet Air Arm made available Barracuda aircraft onto which the Mosquito pilots had quickly to convert. The dummy deck at the Fleet Air Arm airfield at Crail was used for practise landings before the 618 Squadron pilots became the first RAF pilots to land on a carrier, HMS *Rajah*. The Barracudas were not handed back in quite the same condition as they were loaned, because 6 of them were damaged, and Flt Lt MacLean ditched one of them off Troon.

Some idea of the concentrated effort can be gleaned from the fact that, in the 31 days of August, the squadron logged up 401 sorties, totalling over 392 hours, excluding the transfer of aircraft from Wick to Beccles. That was completed between the 23rd and 25th of August.

One of the squadron aircraft, Mosquito DZ537/G was flown down to Farnborough, for fuselage strength tests. On 6th September it was flown to Renfrew, Scotland, for loading trials on the carrier HMS *Implacable,* then returned to Farnborough.

The new crews had no experience of dropping the stores. They were put to making runs over the painted target at Beccles, dropping sashlite bulbs so that the height and distance from target could be measured. All the crews were involved also in using the range at Wells-next-the-Sea, near to Beccles; a total of 68 stores were dropped. That range had the advantage of drying out at low tide, enabling the stores to be recovered, checked and re-used.

Admiral E de F. Renouf accompanied Dr. Barnes Wallis on a visit to the squadron on 20th September. This was the first time that Barnes Wallis had been able to spend time with most of the crews who were to deliver 'his' weapon to a hostile target. In the Ops. Room, he was delighted to accept an invitation to talk about the development of the bouncing bomb. But even those in the audience who could remember their Matric maths. had difficulty in following the profusion of al-gebraic equations with which he soon filled the board. His visit was very timely, in giving that final 'lift' to these busy crews.

The Royal Navy was persuaded, mostly through Admiral Renouf (AMW Ad), to make a battleship available as a target ship, to be moored in Loch Striven – the loch where the *Courbet* had been lo-cated. The battleship HMS *Malaya* was nominated, but at that time, she was part of the fleet of ships that were bombarding the French coast in support of the Allied landings. The Navy was, naturally, not able to say immediately when the ship could be withdrawn from active service and be re-located in Scotland. The aircraft that would make the dummy attacks were ordered to RAF, Dallachy on the Banff coast in mid-September, and Turnberry was brought back into use again. HMS *Malaya* arrived late September in Loch Striven, and deliberately al-tered its ballast to create a list. The effect was to expose more of the lower, armour-plated hull to the impact of the inert stores, so protect-ing its thinner skinned upper hull.

In spite of bad weather and 15 foot waves, attacks on HMS *Malaya* were carried out in the last days of September and into October; more than 70 stores were dropped. The final attacks were carried out on 12th October. Two of the three *Highballs* penetrated the after – and softer – part of the hull, one entering the wardroom flat and the other the Admiral's Pantry. The ship's captain reported that extensive damage would have followed if the stores had been filled with HE. Despite ruining the Admiral's Pantry, the stores were at last performing to expectation.

On 11th October, Warr Off A. R. W. Milne, with his navigator, Flt Sgt E. A. Stubbs, were flying from Beccles to Turnberry in adverse weather. They were attempting to break cloud near the Yorkshire coast, but sadly crashed into a hill near Bramsdale, killing both of them. The aircraft DZ648 was carrying two live stores, so a security cordon had to be thrown around the area, until the Special Police attached to the squadron were able to remove the stores.

There was, initially, some concern as to whether the 5 PRU crews would be able to master deck landing and take-off in the limited time available. They flew to Wick from where they completed deck landing trials on HMS *Implacable* off Scapa Flow in the space of three days.

Meanwhile, back at the ranch, as they say – the Royal Navy, the RAF, de Havillands, Vickers Armstrong and the MAP were all working on the detailed plans for the shipment of aircraft and crews to the Far East. The initial plan to load the entire squadron onto one large aircraft carrier was scrapped, because of inadequate space. Instead it was decided that two escort carriers would be used. An immense amount of dovetailing was going to be needed, including separating the wings from the fuselage, tying in the dates of sailing with the convoy to Gibraltar, loading more than 200 stores, making sure that spares inventories were complete, etc etc. The RAF began to get tetchy with their Navy colleagues, who seemed to the RAF to be unwilling to commit themselves as to which fleet carriers would be assigned. This was merely a reflection of the pressure that was on all concerned – no matter how senior.

Once it became known that the escort carriers *Fencer* and *Striker* would move the squadron, and that they would be sailing at the end of October, 'the decks had to be cleared'. HMS *Malaya* was not returned to service after repairs until 15th October, so a plan to fly the squadron in a formation attack on the Home Fleet, including that ship, – at 12 hours' notice – was abandoned.

Gp Capt Kearny was posted in to 618 Squadron to act as the liaison officer between the squadron, the Royal Navy, the US and Air

Command, South East Asia. He had previously worked with the Fleet Air Arm, so had practical experience of carrier based flying.

Another posting was that of Wg Cdr Hicks, formerly the Flt Lt Security Officer of 618 Squadron, to Air Command, South East Asia, with particular responsibility for ensuring the continuing secrecy of the *Highball* weapon.

That satisfactory progress was being achieved is evident from the TOP SECRET report by the ACAS (OPS) to the Chiefs of Staff on 12th October 1944, in which he says:–

"During my visit to Scotland we held a conference aboard the *Implacable* at which it was stated that it would be a great help to the Navy if we could, in any way, curtail the deck landing programme laid down for 618 Squadron Mosquito crews. I agreed that if the 5 PRU crews carried out the landing trials without difficulty we could afford to forego training the remaining crews until they arrived in South East Asia Command in view of the fact that they have all satisfactorily completed preliminary training in Barracuda aircraft. 5 PRU crews completed their deck landing training with no incident last Tuesday. Incidentally, this was also to be regarded as a test of the deck landing quality of the Mosquito and arrester gear, which were eminently satisfactory. According to the present programme, the squadron should embark in two escort carriers and leave for ACSEA during the first week in November. Altogether a most satisfactory state of affairs...

"We are also taking up at once the question of training replacement crews for 618 Squadron and development of sufficient aircraft to equip the second *Highball* squadron, if it is finally approved. In this connection it should be stated that the weapon has proved to be most satisfactory in trials, and I understand all Naval authorities are very impressed with the high standard of efficiency shown by 618 Squadron in their attacks."[2]

In an exchange of brief signals between Air Ministry and the Commander of Air Command, South East Asia, Air Ministry was told that the Commander-in-Chief, Eastern Forces had signalled the First Sea Lord to the effect that he could not foresee a target which would be accessible to carriers based on Ceylon. The port at which the carriers would discharge their cargoes of aircraft and stores would need heavy lift gear. If that port was Cochin, South India, the rate of unloading would be 4 aircraft per day at best. The aircraft would then be re-assembled and flown to China Bay.

[2]PRO AIR20-1000

The teams of craftsmen from de Havillands worked frantically to dis-assemble the Mosquitos at Renfrew, and to supervise the loading of the airframes onto the Queen Marys road low-loaders. These teams would be facing a long sea journey before being called on again to show their expertise.

Down at the King George V Naval Dock on the Clyde, the pieces of the aircraft were hoisted aboard the two escort carriers and stowed. That work was completed by 28th October. The next day a special train left Beccles for Glasgow with 363 personnel, who, together with the 45 already at Renfrew, would be joining the ships. Doubtless the Masters-at Arms had never piped aboard so many RAF officers as on this occasion.

The two ships left their berths at 11.00 hours on 31st October, and made their way down the Clyde to join the convoy bound for Gibraltar. The carriers put into Gib. on 4th November for 24 hours to refuel and provision. Some squadron personnel were allowed ashore to stretch their legs, before the journey through the Med. and the Suez Canal. The carriers berthed at Trincomalee in Ceylon on 22nd November.

Some 150 personnel were taken to the rest camp at Kiniya, but they were back the following day because of malaria at the camp. One of the ground staff, LAC Harrison, drowned while bathing at Dutch Bay.

The Admiral of the Carrier Force, Trincomalee, visited both carriers to meet 618 Squadron personnel. The next day, 1st December, Hutch and his navigator, French, flew into Columbo, en route for Australia, where they would be making the reception arrangements.

On 4th December, Air Marshal Sir Arthur Garrod, AOC-in-C, South East Asia Command, welcomed the squadron to the Pacific war theatre. He was able to tell them very little of the detailed plans for their future operations, as the operations against the Japanese were very much dictated by the US military and naval commanders.

After taking aboard each carrier 3 Barracuda aircraft for communications between the carriers, *Fencer* and *Striker* joined a convoy comprising a cruiser, 2 destroyers and two other carriers, the *Athlone* and *Battler*. 618 Squadron was on the move again. The convoy was later joined by four more destroyers, and all ships arrived safely in Melbourne on 23rd December. Christmas 1944 was spent in Melbourne, and early in the New Year the slow process of offloading and re-assembly began. That work went on at Fisherman's Bend, from where the aircraft were flown to the squadron's new base

Cover from 618 Squadron's first and only magazine, May 1945.

at RAAF, Narromine, a small airfield outside the city of Sydney.

The routine of long distance navigation and low flying exercises began again. 21 of the aircrew were flown north to the Admiralty Islands, 2° south of the Equator, and part of the Bismarck Archipelago, off Papua New Guinea. The object of that exercise was to give them some experience of the tropical conditions in which they could expect to operate.

The problem with the *Highball* aircraft was that they continued to be classified as TOP SECRET, and so could not land at any old airfield. This was very restrictive. So, in May, 1945, a dozen Mosquito Mk VI FB were shipped out from the UK, then assembled and flight tested at Mascot, before being handed over to the squadron for training use.

One of those Mark VI Mossies, HR 576, was lost on 2nd May, when being air tested from de Havilland Aircraft Pty Ltd Mascot. It exploded and crashed in the Sydney suburbs, killing the pilot, Flt Lt D. G. Rochford and his passenger, LAC Doybell.

There were bigger problems – which led to inactivity at squadron level. The war against the Japanese had achieved a spectacular momentum, and the war zone was moving farther away from the squadron at Narromine. On 25th October, when the squadron was still in the UK, the Americans had fought the battle of Leyte Gulf, which signalled the end of Japanese sea power. They moved on to the second battle for the Philipines, and on 11th January the US Marines had stormed into Manila, the capital.

By the time that the squadron had shaken itself down and declared its readiness, the battle for Iwo Jima was under way. Iwo Jima, in the Volcano Islands, only 760 miles south of Tokyo was invaded by US troops on 19th February.

Operational aircraft carriers were not available on which to embark the squadron for an attack against what remained of the Japanese capital ships. It had been made clear by the Chiefs of Staff that the secret nature of the weapon was not to be compromised by mounting an attack that might turn out to be less than successful, or on a secondary target.

The solution lay in moving the squadron to a forward base from which it could mount an attack against the enemy in one of its home ports. The AOC-in-C, and the UK Air Liaison Mission, had been endeavouring to persuade the US commanders to provide space on a forward airfield, and to assign a suitable target to 618 Squadron. The reply was set out clearly in a report from the RAF Delegation in Washington dated 17th May 1945:–

"In regard to *Highball*, the American Navy left the trials in the hands of the Army Air Force on the grounds that *Highball* would be used in shore-based aircraft and the Army Air Force would therefore be the users. The AAF have carried out trials which were moderately successful. They had one or two bad accidents; one of the stores ricocheted and tore off the tail of the trials aircraft. (An A.26) As a result of this and also of the opinion that they cannot afford to set aside airfield space in the Pacific for specialist squadrons that may or may not ever come into operation, they have dropped the *Highball* proposition. Lutzenheiser felt that, owing to the considerable damage now being sustained by the American fleet from suicide bombers, the American Navy would be loathe to disclose *Highball* at present on the grounds that it might provide the Japanese with yet a further formidable weapon. He stated, however, that the AAF were very optimistic about the termination of the war against Japan and he would not oppose the use of *Highball* on the grounds of disclosure to the Japanese but he stressed the point that, owing to the shortage of airfield accommodation, it would be most undesirable to set aside airfield space for a specialist squadron which, owing to the lack of suitable targets, might never come into operation."

"From the above, it appears probable that the American Navy would oppose the use of *Highball* on the grounds of disclosure, the American Air Force on the grounds of lack of airfield accommodation. It is unlikley, therefore, that the Americans would oppose a suggestion to withdraw 618 Squadron from the Pacific."[3]

When news of this got to the squadron there was a general feeling that the Americans were saying; "This is our war, and we're winning it our way. We don't need your help."

In June, the UK Air Liaison Mission returned from the UK, where it had been seeking employment for the squadron, with the news that the squadron's association with the British Pacific Fleet would cease, and that there was no future for the squadron in the South West Pacific theatre.

Morale hit an all time low. The Adjutant, Flt Lt Hawley, who had been with the squadron through all its trials and tribulations, found

[3]PRO AIR 15-442

some employment by offering the local farmers help with bringing in the harvest. It was also a small way to repay some of the great hospitality that had been showered on the squadron personnel.

VE Day was a time for rejoicing in Australia as in the rest of the free world, even though the war against Japan continued. Hutch, pulling rank, decided that he would make a spectacular contribution to the celebrations in the town of Narromine. He would taxy one of the squadron's Barracuda aircraft into the town. This novel idea came to grief when he took a short cut across the local golf course, and the aircraft ran out of brake pressure. There is no record of what the golfers said about the completely unique hazard that the tyres would have created along the fairways!

On 29th June 1945 Admiral Portal, the Commander of the British Pacific Fleet, took the unusual step of coming personally to Narromine where all the squadron was assembled. He read a signal that had been sent from the Vice Chief of Air Staff, London:–

"Please convey to the CO and all ranks of 618 Squadron good wishes from the Air Staff and regrets that circumstances have again compelled us to disband the squadron after a long period of tedious waiting and before they have had an opportunity to fulfil the task for which they were selected and worked so hard. I am sure that, had they been given the opportunity we all hoped for, they would have ac-quitted themselves with distinction. Nevertheless, their work has not been fruitless. As a result of the trials carried out by personnel of 618 Squadron since its formation, we have been able to develop a weapon which may have great value in the future.

The weapon still remains in reserve, and all personnel should be impressed, before dispersal, for continued need for security on this subject".[4]

Nothing to do but to pack our bags and go.[5]

On 19th June, Flg Off E. G. Bell and Flt Lt E. B. Sillito, a PR crew, were killed at Benall, Victoria. Their aircraft, NS 735, was seen in a vertical dive from which it did not recover.

Next month, on 27th July, another flying accident claimed the lives of Sqn Ldr J. S. "Sammy" McGoldrick and Hutch's navigator,

[4]PRO AIR 27-2130
[5]The first atomic bomb was dropped on Japan in August, and VJ Day was celebrated on 15th August 1945

Flt Lt Francis French. Their Mosquito, a Mk VI HR614, crashed just ouside the town of Narromine. The official report said that no definite cause had been established, but one of his colleagues recalls that Sammy McGoldrick was buzzing the airfield before going to Sydney on home leave.

Squadron personnel had begun to disperse in July. The only two remaining as 'nightwatchmen' at RAAF, Narromine to see in the New Year 1946 were Flt Lt R. A. Payne, Signals, and Flg Off F. B. Boreham, a navigator.

Other casualties – in the immediate aftermath of the disperal of the crews – were Flt Lt Frankie Foss, who crashed at Brunei, possibly while doing low level aerobatics, Joe Massey who was killed in a road accident in Singapore, and Flt Lt 'Nipper' MacLean, who was shot by a sniper in Jakarta.

Special equipment that was consigned for local destruction was escorted to Sydney, where it was broken up and shipped in Navy launches to "somewhere in the South Pacific Ocean," where it was unceremoniously consigned thereto. S/L T. J. Rose, MBE, Armaments, and Flt Lt Ketch, Security, witnessed this "tragic performance" as described in the Squadron Operations Record.

Then the *Highball* stores that were stored near Sydney were statically exploded, causing a certain amount of discomfort to local housewives.

Some of the secret equipment was loaded aboard the UK-bound SS *Mauretania* under the control of Wg Cdr Moore. A number of deputations visited the unit in October to see what was available as 'pickings', but with the war over, no great interest seemed to exist. Then as the year came to a close, all remaining serviceable equipment, except spares for 2 Mosquito Mark XVI's, was packed for shipment to 389 MU, Singapore.

618 Squadron had started with great promise of achieving at sea success as great or even greater than its sister squadron, 617 Squadron, had achieved on land. Alas, it was not to be.

Yet there was a small posse of 618 Squadron air and ground crew, who made an indelible mark on the German U-boat fleet, and on their ships that operated within the comparative safety to the Germans of the coast of Occupied France.

S/Ldr McGoldrick, S/Ldr Binks, W/Cdr Hutchinson and S/Ldr Melville-Jackson. 618 Squadron at Narrowmine, Australia, 1945.

L to R. J.S. Boyd, Don Maynard, Jackie Price and Bertie Umbers.

618 Squadron pilots learning to fly off aircraft carriers. Training on Albatros aircraft.

CHAPTER 9

New Artillery of the Sea

While the reformed 618 Squadron had travelled with its aircraft to the other side of the world – only to suffer its second disappointment – a small detachment had been brought together in Cornwall to go into action with another unusual weapon mounted in a Mosquito aircraft.

The Molins Manufacturing Co. Ltd. was a prominent business in the cigarette machine industry. It had turned over part of its manufacturing capacity to the production of armaments, and had developed a 57 mm calibre, automatic loading, anti-tank weapon, that fired a 6-lb warhead. The Military decided, however, to use the more powerful 80 mm howitzer that was also becoming available.

In March 1943, de Havilland had been asked to investigate the possibility of installing this six-pounder gun into a Mosquito. They responded by cutting the front section from a crashed Mosquito, installing the field gun and setting it up on the Hatfield firing butts at the end of April. The firing was filmed by the Ministry of Aircraft Production, who were thus able to study the recoil effects. The idea seemed to be practicable.

In May de Havillands used another crashed aircraft to set up a mock installation to work out, with Molins, how the ammunition loading and feeding into the breech block might be arranged. Meanwhile, they were modifying a Mark VI F version HJ 732 into which the gun and its ammunition rack was to be mounted. An order was placed by MAP for 30 of this variant, the Mosquito Mark XVIII – the 'Tsetse'.

After firing trials at Hatfield, that prototype was delivered to the A. & AEE (Aircraft & Armaments Experimental Establishment) at Boscombe Down. There, the firing trials encountered problems with the ammunition feed, so the aircraft had to go back to Hatfield for minor modification. But the installation was showing itself to be practical, and was to be yet another weapon in the war against the U-boats. This one was specifically to carry out high speed attacks on the U-boats close into their heavily defended ports. This called for fitting extra armour plating within the engine cowlings, around the nose and over the cockpit floor.

Firing trials at Boscombe Down and at Exeter showed that this gun could perform with great accuracy, and that the wear on the rifling of the gun barrel – at three to five hundred rounds – was acceptable. de Havillands were able to fit an additional 35 gallon tank in the fuselage to extend the range of the aircraft over the Bay of Biscay.

The Mark XVIII aircraft were slow in coming off the production line, due simply to the weight of orders for the Wooden Wonder from all the Commands. The first two aircraft were not ready for operational use until mid October 1943. Then some aircrew with experience of operating in enemy coastal waters were needed to fly these two aircraft operationally. The fighter and ship-busting squadrons of Coastal Command were equipped with Beaufighters, so the only likely sources of experienced Mosquito aircrew within Coastal were the met. flight, and the PR squadrons. Then someone remembered that some of 618 Squadron had been recruited from those fighter/ship-busting squadrons. The Command Postings Officer was instructed to track some of them down.

Sqn Ldr Charlie Rose, DFC, DFM. was still with the small nucleus of air and ground crew of 618 Squadron in the north of Scotland. Hutch was persuaded to release him to command a newly formed small unit to fly this new piece of airborne artillery. Charlie Rose, with a new navigator, Sgt Cowley, were flown down to Boscombe Down to be briefed by the pilots who had test flown this new variant, and had evolved a technique for using the gun. From there they flew the first operational aircraft to RAF Predannack, on the most southerly tip of Cornwall.

Thirty four ground staff from 618 Squadron came down by rail at the beginning of October 1943. This new unit was designated as 618 Squadron Special Detachment – thus ensuring that the personnel would be available to 618 Squadron should they be required. No. 248 Fighter (Beaufighter) Squadron, Coastal Command, was one of the units then based at Predannack , and 618 Squadron SD were attached for pay, rations and discipline to 248 Squadron.

When most of the crews were dispersed from Skitten, Flg Off 'Hilly' Hilliard and his navigator, Warr Off Jimmy Hoyle were returned to 235 Squadron, and the Beaufighter. Plt Off B. C. 'Robbie' Roberts and Flt Sgt F. G. Winsor were posted to 248 Squadron. Flt Lt E. H. Jeffreys DFC and the other Warr Off Burden DA 968 were

posted to RAF Benson, then were formally posted to 248 Squadron
on 1st March 1944. Flg Off Al Bonnett's navigator, Warr Off Denny
Burden, had been hospitalized; his new navigator was Plt Off McD
'Pickles' McNicol, who was posted into 618 Squadron on 19th
September and the same day posted out to join Al Bonnett, at RAF
Benson. Bonnett had reached 540 PRU Squadron via a ten-day
attachment to 236 Squadron. Flg Off DJ Doug Turner and the author
were also posted to 540 Squadron, RAF Benson.

The remainder of this story is largely autobiographical, drawing as
it does on the experiences of the author among the small number of
618 Squadron who flew the Mark XVIII Mosquito.

Having delivered off at RAF Shawbury the *Highball* aircraft we
got a lift to RAF Benson, the Photographic Reconnaissance Group
airfield near to the Photographic Interpretation Unit at RAF Medmenham, in Oxfordshire. We were told that we would be flying a
new PR Mosquito to North Africa by way of Italy; we would do a
line overlap run down the west coast of Italy. That meant flying in a
straight line, so that the cameras in the belly of the aircraft could take
a series of black and white pictures, each of which slightly overlapped
the previous one.

We were given our jabs for tropical service, and seven days leave.
Then we would air-test this sparklingly new pale blue Mosquito for
three hours before the operational sortie. The air-test meant a climb
to 30,000 feet, which was a phenomenal height to us who were accus-
tomed to operating down near the wave tops. At the end of the test,
we spiralled down over Benson, mostly in cloud, and were astounded
to pass through formations of Boeing Flying Fortresses of the USAAF
that were setting out on a daylight raid over the Continent.

A few days later we were blindfolded and led into the back of a
five-ton truck. When the blindfold was removed we were in front of
an elegant mansion that housed the PIU, the blindfold being a pre-
caution against our being able to pinpoint the place should we be
captured. We were particularly impressed by the skill of the inter-
preters, mostly young WAAF officers, in following particular ships
from indistinct photos taken at differing angles. The high level prints
of the ships in the northern Norwegian fjords looked much like the
layouts we had been working on at Skitten.

Then we reported to the Ops Room for briefing on the flight to the
Middle East, – to be told by the Senior Controller that we were stood

down from that mission. We went across to the station adjutant who told us that he'd had a signal to the effect that we were required at RAF Predannack, in Cornwall – to report to a Sqn Ldr C. F. Rose.

We were met at Helston station by the truck from the RAF camp, and taken to the Officers Mess. There was the familiar face of Charlie Rose, with his bright blue laughing eyes. Al Bonnet and Pickles McNicol, and Hilly and Jimmy Hoyle were also on their way to make up the aircrew complement of 618 Squadron Special Detachment. Charlie was full of excitement as he poured forth his description of this weapon and all its possibilities. He was less enthusiastic about the support that was being offered to us. There were Mosquitos on the airfield that belonged to a Fighter Command squadron. The CO of 248 Squadron had just got word that they would soon start to replace their Beaufighters with Mosquitos, but for the time being they couldn't help with spares, etc.

Charlie had acquired a Standard Eight van as the detachment transport, and we had been allocated a small hangar and a caravan at a far dispersal point. He decided that we should go over to station headquarters to meet the station commander, Wg Cdr P. Lawton, DFC. He was politely curt, and seemed almost resentful of our presence at Predannack. He told us that the signal that he had received said that a detachment of 618 Squadron would be flying experimental operations with a secret weapon fitted in a Mosquito. "Only those personnel who had a reason to see the aircraft should be permitted to do so, and the unit should be housed away from other units." He obviously expected Charlie to fill him in on all the details, which Charlie was not about to do. The short interview concluded with the C.O. telling us that there was no surplus servicing equipment on the airfield, so we had better tell Coastal Command HQ what we would need. In other words, "You're on your own".

Then we went to the our flight office, an old caravan parked beside the small hanger. But within the hanger was Mosquito Mk XVIII HX902, from the nose of which protruded the barrel of the 57mm Molins gun. Charlie's enthusiasm was infectious, and we were all itching to get started. The next two aircraft, HX 903 and HX 904 would be ready for collection in a matter of days.

Charlie read out the copy of the Operational Order which had been sent on 19th October by SASO Coastal Command to the AOC 19 Group:–

"Three Mosquitos are to be attached to 248 Squadron, RAF

Predannack for operational trials. At least four attacks on U-boats are required to enable an assessment of future policy for this weapon.

"The aircraft will patrol specific areas. The patrol areas are normally:–

A 46.32N 04.25W along a Bearing of 360°T to the Coast,
B 46.32N 04.52W along a Bearing of 039°T to the Coast,
C 46.15N 03.17W along a Bearing of 030°T to the Coast,
D 45.40N 03.07W along a Bearing of 061°T to the Coast,
E 45.27N 03.00W along a Bearing of 078°T to the Coast,
F 45.02N 02.29W along a Bearing of 049°T to the Coast,
G 44.33N 02.19W along a Bearing of 029°T to the Coast.

"Information will be telephoned daily by this Headquarters on Scrambler line, indicating which of these patrols are to be flown, e.g. 'Two inward bound U-boats expected line C tomorrow 5th November from 11.00 hours onwards'.

"It is probable that U-boats time their departure from Bay ports so as to pass through the mine-swept channels on the surface at night. Even if they do submerge on reaching the westward end of the channels, it may be possible to take them by surprise still on the surface at first light. Notice will sometimes be short and it is therefore essential that the detachment should be organised so as to be able to operate one aircraft at very short notice."

"The aircraft will normally patrol singly during daylight, but pilots must be prepared to take off or land in the dark."

"The detachment will maintain one aircraft and one crew at one hour's readiness, the remaining aircraft to be prepared to take off for operations if available within the same length of time"

signed SASO, HQCC.[1] (See map page 142.)

RAF Predannack was a busy operational airfield, but with no Officers Mess within the airfield. Two hotels on the cliff edge had been requisitioned, one immediately outside the village of Mullion. That was the Polurrian Hotel, a very elegant white building with grounds that led onto the cliff path. To the east the road led from the village up to the airfield; to the west to the large sandy cove of Polurrian Beach. Further west, overlooking an equally attractive beach was the Poldhu Hotel, in which the Coastal Command English, Polish and Czech officers were housed.

[1] PRO AIR 20-1254

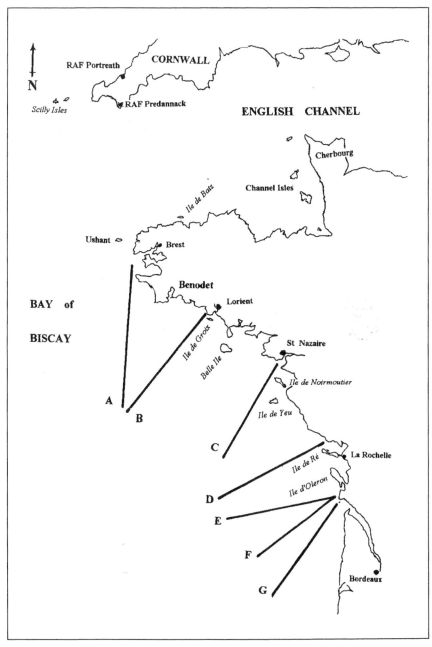

Mine-swept channels A to G leading from the Bay of Biscay to the German U-boat bases. Water depth in channels was too shallow to permit U-boats to crash-dive if attacked.

A Mosquito FB Mk XVIII of 618 Squadron Special Detachment – October 1943. (RAF Museum)

Mosquito Mk XVIII "O" of No 618 Squadron Special Detachment in D-Day markings.

Sqdn Ldr 'Tony' Phillips, DSO, DFC briefly CO of 618 Squadron Special Detachment, before becoming CO of 248 Squadron. (author)

The 'emblem' of 618 Squadron Special Detachment, devised by Flt Sgt Cowley. His pilot, Sqn Ldr C. F. Rose, DFC, DFM was a Guernseyman. A formal squadron badge was never granted to 618 Squadron.

ABOVE: *The nose of a Tsetse Mosquito Mk XVIII showing muzzle of Molins 57mm artillery gun below the four Browning .303 machine guns.* (author)

LEFT: *A corporal armourer holding a 57mm shell below the aircraft.*

L to R. Flg Off Curtis DFC, Flg Off Thomson DFC, Sqn Ldr Phillips, DSO, DFC, Flg Off Turner DFC. (Doug Turner)

Flg Off Doug Turner DFC. (author)

*Flg Off Al Bonnett, RCAF.
(*Tim Murray*)*

Hilly Hilliard and Jimmy Hoyle, June 1996.

We were initially accommodated in the Polurrian Hotel, along with the members of 111 Fighter Squadron, then on Typhoons, and a Mosquito squadron.

The mess was about ten minutes from camp, using up valuable minutes against the requirement to have one aircraft ready to take off at one hour's notice, 24 hours a day. That left little time for briefing, preparing a flight plan, getting into full flying kit and getting aboard the aircraft. It also meant that, in theory, the stand-by crew could not move far from a telephone nor should they enjoy a few pints in the mess. Theory and practise are seldom the same thing; we adapted our life style, and enjoyed life. But we were always ready to respond to those brief operational orders.

We could hardly contain our excitement at the prospect of, first of all, trying out this flying field gun, and then taking it out on the first ops. trip. We all had a great admiration for the power and performance of the Mosquito. What will this novel weaponry enable us to do against the U-boat?

This variant of the Mosquito was quickly christened the *Tsetse* from the African insect similar to and just as harmful as the Mosquito. The arc-shaped magazine, holding 24 rounds of 57 mm armour plated HE shells capped with Tracer, was positioned vertically about midship, feeding into the breech block. The breech block was behind the crew, and the barrel extended below the floor of the cockpit, the muzzle protruding below the fairing of the nose. The 4 Browning .303 mm front guns, that had been retained, projected beyond the nose cone, above the muzzle of the big gun.

All these guns were sighted through one reflector sight, the firing buttons being on the control column. The big gun had a muzzle velocity of 2,950 feet per second. (For the technically minded, the trajectory of the shell was very flat when fired in level flight. The gun was synchronised so that the sight coincided with the line of flight at 500 and 1,000 yards, the line of sight being 10 inches above the line of sight at 750 yards.)

The optimum angle of dive was 30 degrees below the horizontal, and the ideal range at which to open fire was 1,800 to 1,500 yards. It was necessary to sight separately each round, with fresh firing pressure applied each time. It was possible to fire up to 6 rounds in a dive, but the last shot should be fired while the aircraft is no nearer the target than 500 yards.

A surfaced submarine is a difficult target to hit. Its low profile, a narrow beam and effective sea-camouflage effectively cut back the target size, and it could turn fast. There are only seconds to get into position to attack.

The direction of attack was critical if full advantage was to be taken of the destructive effect within the hull of the armour-piercing solid warhead. The most effective direction was within 15 degrees of either ahead or astern, i.e. 15° off the line through the length of the U-boat, aiming at the waterline. If an attack exactly up or down the track of the U-boat had to be made, the angle of the dive had to be increased to 35° and the pilot had to aim short of the conning tower.

The reason for aiming at the waterline, rather than at the hull or superstructure, was that after the shell entered the sea, the increased resistance of the water would cause the shell to change its flight path to run parallel to, and several feet below, the surface. The shell would then puncture the hull, making a hole of 6″ to 12″ in diameter, and if it encountered solid metal, such as an engine block, it would ricochet before exiting the hull through a similar sized hole. The inrush of water would quickly de-stabilise the U-boat, which could be fatal in the shallow waters off the French Biscay coast. The theory was sound.

The first time that we fired the gun was electrifying. The noise was deafening, the flame that accompanied the shell from the barrel enveloped the aircraft, and there was a robust jolt as the shell set off towards the target. That jolt was, in fact, the aircraft being propelled backwards for a microsecond by the recoil of the gun. The proof of this was demonstrated on one occasion, when we were returning as the leader in formation with Mosquito escorts after an uneventful patrol. We decided to fire a series of shots in level flight at normal cruising. None of the pilots in the formation adjusted throttles, yet very quickly we were overtaken by the aircraft on our port and starboard.

The second surprise was the clanging thuds below our armour plated seats as the breech block withdrew the spent cartridge and rammed home the next live round. The nearest equivalent to that sensation was that of an anti-aircraft shell exploding just below the aircraft, sending shrapnel clanging into the steel plates.

Now the search began to find the U-boats.

A couple of days after the second Mossie arrived, the first operational flight was made into the Bay of Biscay on 24th October 1943, by Charlie Rose and Al Bonnett. No suitable target presented itself, but we had shown that we were ready. But it was then decided that two 50 gallon drop-tanks should be fitted to give a greater range – of 1,260 n.ms. at a cruising speed of 210 knots. But that extra weight had to be compensated by removing some of the armour plating, and the rate of fire was fine-tuned. All that work was carried out by 3rd November and Charlie Rose was able to notify 19 Group that 618 Squadron Special Detachment was operational with three aircraft and four crews.

The words of the station commander about the lack of help was borne out when we needed to borrow a pair of jacks to do a wheel change. Chiefy was told by the Fighter Mosquito squadron maintenance that their jacks could not be spared, so Charlie decided to wait till late evening, then we would take the Standard van, with ropes aboard, round to their hangar. There, we fumbled around in the dark, pushing the jacks out, to be roped to the back of the van, before towing them back to our flights. Later, the jacks were silently put back where they came from.

We weren't kept hanging around, for the day after we declared our readiness, the 4th November, the order came through from Group that two aircraft were to be airborne at 08.00 hours to proceed to Point A. Briefing was simply a matter of picking up the Very cartridges of the colours of the day, and the met. report. After one of those great aircrew breakfasts of sausage, egg and bacon, we were off in the Standard Eight to flights, and at 08.00 Charlie Rose and Flt Sgt Cowley in HX 902, and Doug Turner and I in HX 903 were airborne and heading south. At about 30 feet above a slight sea, and spaced about 100 yards apart, we passed outside radar range of Ushant Light, off Brest. A slight alteration of course and a check on the wind speed and direction as we headed uneventfully to Point A – an unmarked point on a grey ocean. The cloud base was about 5,000 feet – ideal if we were to sight the U-boat; with enough height from which to start the dive, without losing sight of the target, but providing useful cloud cover if we were attacked by German fighters from the nearby airfields.

We reached our ETA, and Charlie called: "Climbing now". We opened throttles and climbed to 3,000 feet. A quick search of the sea 360 degrees around us revealed only one large trawler. Charlie called:

"You stand off – I'm going to have a close look at that". We stood off – searching for the U-boat, and watching the horizon and cloud for any pouncing fighters.

"Can't see any fishing nets, and there aren't any seagulls around her, so she's not fishing. Probably keeping watch for the likes of us. She'll have some signal to tell the U-boat to keep submerged, I bet. So, we're going to put paid to that." said Charlie.

"I'll go first. You take some photos as I go in, so that we can see what happens as we fire. Then you go in, and we'll watch you".

"Roger. Good luck" replied Doug, as we continued to circle.

Charlie climbed as he manoeuvred into a position to attack from the port bow of the trawler. Then, the aircraft nose went down as he began his dive at 30 degrees. We saw the Mossie momentarily enveloped in flame as he fired off two shots. Then as HX 902 started to level out at about 300 feet, a trail of light grey smoke appeared from behind the port wing. In startled horror we watched Charlie's aircraft cross over the trawler and continue a gentle dive. Without a sound on the r/t, the aircraft hit the calm sea.

Doug immediately dived to where the white water of the giant splash was starting to subside; we were waiting to see perhaps the dinghy start to inflate, or one of the crew floating in the water. There was no sign of life. We had no idea what had caused that fatal crash. Flying back to the trawler, the crew could be seen staring at the spot where the Mossie had crashed – but they made no attempt to fire any light weapons. It was possible that the shots that Charlie had fired had done mortal damage to the trawler, or even that his Mossie had been hit by a ricochet of one of the shells he had fired.

Doug Turner and I returned to Predannack with heavy hearts. 618 Squadron had lost two good men, one of them a much decorated and highly skilled pilot, one who had shown himself in every way to be a first class leader of men.

Back at flights the news was received in stunned silence. All of us, when serving on other squadrons, had lost friends, and the ground crew had waited in vain for their aircraft to come back. But Charlie was someone special. A commander, who would 'borrow' equipment at night, then go off to make a brew for the ground crew while they worked feverishly to get the maintenance done in time to return the equipment before daylight, so that he could be on stand-by at first light. Charlie knew that these ground crew had that same pride in "their" Mossies that pervaded all good operational squadrons. But the first time that the *Tsetse* was taken into battle the enemy had won.

The balance was to be redressed very quickly. On 7th November, Flg Off Al Bonnett and his navigator, Flg Off 'Pickles' McNicol, flying "I"/HX903, were sent out to a potential rendezvous with a returning U-boat, along Channel B. Flying at sea level, they passed west of Ushant, then altered course to port. Arriving at Point B, Bonnett turned onto 039° and climbed to 300 feet. Minutes later – to their astonishment and delight – they spotted a U-boat on the surface off to port. It was on the same heading, and making full speed judging by the length of its wake.

Al Bonnett put the aircraft into a climbing turn, to get quickly to 1,500 feet and to come out of the mid-morning sun. "Don't lose sight of him," Al called to Pickles, who was scrambling for his hand-held camera at the bottom of his nav. bag. The U-boat had seen them and was starting a series of high speed turns.

Then Al Bonnett put "I" into the 30° dive, lined up on the waterline just below the conning tower, and fired. The flame and the thumping noise were all lost in the concentration of keeping the line of flight, and aiming steadily for the next 7 shots which he managed to loose off before pulling out at about 200 feet. At least one shell penetrated the hull between the conning tower and the gun platform, and others hit the hull aft of the tower. The guns on the deck of the U-boat were firing continuously, and McNicol could see the gunners at close range as the Mossie flew across at 340 knots.

The splashes from the other shells hitting the water were still visible as Bonnett started his second run. The flak was very accurate, and they felt at least one shell strike the aircraft. But, during the second diving run, the 57 mm gun jammed. Bonnett could only blaze away with the four .303 Brownings, seeing strikes on the hull.

Yellow smoke was seen to be coming from the U-boat, but as the main weapon was not functioning, Bonnett abandoned any further attacks and turned westwards for Predannack. He landed safely at 11.30 hours with a punctured oil tank.

As the aircraft taxied into the dispersal, someone shouted that the gun had been fired. Soon, everyone on 618 Squadron SD was waiting for Pickles and Al to climb down through the hatch. They all had to have the story before Al drove off to the Ops Room for debriefing.

The second operational sortie by the squadron since its formation nearly eight months earlier had been successful.

The U-boat was, in fact, U-123 – a type IXB, on its thirteenth patrol, and commanded by Oberleutnant von Schroeter, who later became a Vice Admiral in the Bundsmarine.

The three crews, Turner and Curtis, Bonnett and McNicol and Hilliard and Hoyle, carried out almost daily anti-submarine patrols, either singly or as a pair.

A somewhat different order came down from 19 Group on 16th November. An LST (Landing Ship Tanks), presumably one in a convoy coming from North America, had been abandoned in rough weather in the Western Approaches, and was drifting towards the enemy coast. That presented a security risk, as the invasion forces were beginning to be mustered. Air searches so far were unsuccessful. So two *Tsetse* Mosquitos would carry out a square search, in the vicinity of its last known position, to find and destroy it. The Group Navigation Officer had obligingly worked out the detailed square search pattern that should be followed.

Curtis and Hoyle, the two navigators, considered the pattern and concluded that it was not the correct one to follow. Using info. from the Met. office on wind speeds and direction since the last known position some three days earlier, they constructed an elongated oblong search pattern, starting from some 10 miles upwind of the last position, south west of Ushant.

In the search area, the sky was overcast, eight eighths at below 2,000 feet. The two aircraft flew parallel tracks at maximum visual distance. Both navigators maintained plots but Curtis, as leader, gave the turning signals on the Aldis lamp. Under that grey sky, the grey sea was flecked with the white tops of the waves, and somewhere in amongst those waves was a grey silent ship.

All eyes were being strained, realising from experience that imagination can suggest non-existent shapes as one's eyes get more tired. Two minutes, then turn 90° port, five minutes before another 90° turn, then after two more minutes, another turn to port and a longer run as the oblong extended, and so on.

Suddenly, Doug Turner shouted that he had seen the target, but it was lost to sight before Des Curtis could change his line of vision. They came round in a gentle turn, Des noting the time so that the navigation could be kept up later. There was the ship, wallowing but with its bow pointed along the track the two navigators had predicted.

With one aircraft standing off and keeping watch for JU88's or FW Condors, the other made a steady run from below the cloud base, firing without haste. Each Mosquito fired most of its 24 rounds. As the shells were armour piercing, without HE, no explosions were seen; the intention being to riddle the hull with 12 inch diameter holes. The photographs taken by the navigators showed that many direct hits were obtained. The results brought a telegram of congratulations from the Air Officer Commanding-in-Chief, Coastal Command.

The following day, these same crews, Turner/Curtis in "I" HX903 and Hilliard/Hoyle in "E" HX904, made an early morning run along one of the mine swept channels. There was no U-boat, but they flew past a destroyer and three armed trawlers.

Things were changing in several ways.

The German Naval High Command had been taken unawares by the ferocity of the attack by Al Bonnett, so close in to the U-boat base. Protection in the form of surface warships would have to be provided for the incoming and outgoing U-boats during their passage out to the open sea.

Coastal Command and other commands now had the resources in terms of aircraft and crews to fly many more patrols right on the French coast and against the ports. The Atlantic coastline was being criss-crossed by a variety of Allied aircraft, including the Mosquito squadron at Predannack.

248 Squadron at Predannack were starting to take delivery of the Mosquito Mark VI FB, and the crews had to be converted from Beaufighters. Wg Cdr Barron was appointed CO of 248 Squadron on 7th November. On 9th, Sqn Ldr A. J. Phillips, DFC and Flg Off R. W. Thomson were posted in to 618 Squadron SD, as replacements for Charlie Rose and Flt Sgt Cowley, but two weeks later were transferred to 248 Squadron Mosquito Conversion Flight; Phillips as CO. Early in December, 618 Squadron sent some of its – by then – supernumerary crews to train the crews and to fly with them on operations. Those crews were Flg Off Hamlett and Warr Off Mudd, Flg Off's Foss and Groome, and Flt Sgts Massey and Fletcher. Sqn Ldr Phillips and Flg Off Thomson came back to the Special Detachment at the beginning of 1944.

Two of the *Tsetse* Mosquitos (Phillips and Turner), were on patrol on 7th January when they came across a Lorient type trawler and a fishing boat – both stationary but with no nets visible. While examining these craft, the crews saw a patch of very calm bright green water with 'luminous bubbles' rising from what appeared to be a depth of some 20 to 30 feet. They kept watch for 23 minutes but saw no other activity. One possibility was that the trawlers were acting as markers/look-outs for the U-boats, and had spotted the aircraft in sufficient time to warn the U-boat to lie low.

The Commander-in-Chief, Coastal Command, Air Chief Marshal Sir Sholto Douglas came to see the Special Detachment during his tour of RAF Predannack on 1st February.

During our stay at RAF Predannack, Wimpey, the construction company, was engaged in extending one of the runways, using mostly Irish labour. One of the ground crew came in to the caravan and said that in the pub in Mullion one of the labourers had boasted that if the runway on the end of which they were working was brought into use – even during a few minutes while the wind was veering or backing – the workforce got danger money. That danger money was more than Flying Officers were getting as a day's pay including flying pay. So the rule became: "If you're taking off towards the contractors, lift off as late as possible, and make them earn their money!"

Newly promoted Flt Lt's Foss and Groome, with Plt Off Fletcher and Flt Sgt Massey completed their attachment to 248 Squadron and returned to 618 Squadron at Wick. Flg Off 'Hammy' Hamlett and his navigator, Warr Off Bert Mudd, joined the *Tsetse* Special Detachment.

Then, on 16th February 248 Squadron and 618 Squadron SD were transferred across the Cornish peninsular to RAF Portreath – an already busy airfield, one of its functions being the Overseas Aircraft Despatch Unit, from where aircraft and personnel were moved to and from Gibraltar and North Africa.

The increased protection being afforded to the U-boats meant that the *Tsetse* aircraft were becoming very vulnerable to shore and naval flak and the air cover provided from nearby air bases. Hitherto, the

*Tsetse*s of 618 Squadron Special Detachment had carried out patrols alone along the channels and on the coast. It was decided that the *Tsetse* aircraft should be escorted – usually by Mosquitos of 248 Squadron – which would attack escort vessels and enemy aircraft.

Flt Lt Jeffreys DFC and Flg Off Burden had been detached to 248 Squadron from 618 – they were in a 'party' that had a ding-dong battle on 10th March, 1944. The battle opened when Sqn Ldr Tony Phillips in *Tsetse* "E" and Doug Turner in "L", with an escort of 4 Mosquito Mk VI FB of 248 Squadron were despatched to an area about 30 miles north of Gijon on the Spanish coast. The cloud base was 1,500 feet, 8-10 miles visiblity. The formation was flying on a course of 175° at 100 feet when a naval force was sighted. Almost immediately, one of the escorts called "Bandits at 2 o'clock – 1500 feet". There were about 8 or 10 JU88's/JU188's. Tony Phillips ordered a climb to cloud base, circling the ships but at one point about 4 miles from them. The 4 Mossie escorts made a head-on attack on the JU88's, one of which immediately fell into the sea.

A second JU88 was hit and turned towards the naval force, but Flt Sgt Tonge stayed with it and another burst from his cannons sent a sheet of flame from the starboard engine; the enemy aircraft went into the sea in flames. Flg Off Forrest, another of the escort, registered hits on a JU88, which escaped into cloud.

Jeffreys had stayed with the *Tsetse*s as they were identifying the naval targets and moving into position for an attack. He spotted a JU 88 closing towards the *Tsetse*s, and opening his throttles, climbed to make a head-on attack on the enemy. He estimated that he closed to 30 feet before breaking. He later reported that smoke was seen coming from it. In turn, Jeffreys' aircraft was twice attacked, and in climbing away, he lost contact with the rest of the Mosquito force.

Down below, the naval force comprised four Elbing class destroyers escorting a surfaced U-boat; the U-boat was of the 1,600 ton class. They were steering due East at about 12 knots. "E" made four attacks on the U-boat, and "L" two, the second in formation with "E". Two hits were claimed on the bows and four near the conning tower. Strangely the flak from the U-boat and its destroyers was light at first, but was intense during the later runs.

As they were climbing away from the second attack, Tony Phillips spotted a JU88 making for cloud cover. With the superior speed of the Mossie he came up behind the enemy, levelled off and – with remarkable accuracy – fired four shots from the 57mm gun. One of those literally tore an engine from the JU88, which spiralled down to the sea. Tony Phillips climbed to 7,000 feet to transmit, in order that other anti-submarine aircraft could home on this target. His transmission, heard by the WAAF back at Portrteath, went:

Mary had a little lamb
Wasn't the doctor surprised
The lamb, in fact, was a little boy
So it had to be circumcised.

The girls on duty seemed to think that was good, coming from a senior officer.

Two Liberators had arrived on the scene just before the Mosquitos had to set off – all returning safely to base.

On 21st March, two *Tsetse*s, "L", Turner, and "I" (pilot not known) with 4 fighter escorts were on patrol in the north Spanish coast area when they came across a 1,500 ton merchant vessel which was set on fire. It subsequently sank. One of the escorting Mosquitos V (LR367) Flt Sgt Mowat and Flg Off Orr, was hit by the flak, and nearly made it back to Cornwall. The aircraft ditched 25 miles of the Lizard, and both were drowned. One of the escorting Mosquitos was crewed by Flt Lt Cobbledick and Flg Off Belcher, who later joined 618 Squadron at Wick.

Two days later, flying "L", Hilly Hilliard saw three JU88's approach to attack, but they were driven off by the Mossie escorts.

When the bars in the messes closed, the *Tsetse* crews who were on stand-by went down the hill – off the station – to the Sector Ops block, to sleep in two tier bunks in a small rest-room. In the early hours of 25th March, the two *Tsetse* crews were awoken. A signal from Group ordered them to Point C at 0845. Doug Turner and Des Curtis in "L" and, Hilly Hilliard and Jimmy Hoyle in "I", set off in company with four Mosquitos of 248 Squadron. On ETA they turned onto a track of 030° which would bring them onto the west side of the Ile d' Yeu, and to the mouth of the harbour at La Pallice.

The two *Tsetse*s in tight formation, with the escorts as outriders, were skimming the wave tops over a calm sea, on a bright but hazy Spring morning. Then, on the horizon dead ahead, the small but unmistakeable shapes of ships.

"Tally Ho. Target dead ahead. Climbing to 1500 feet NOW",

Doug Turner called. The adrenalin started flowing, excitement being mixed with the fear of coming to sticky end in the sea. The formation extended its width to give space as the attack developed. The first ship to be recognised was a destroyer, then two armed minesweepers. A U-boat was in the centre of this trio of escorts.

Turner and Hilliard turned to starboard to position themselves in the sun. It was 09.15 as the attack began. The pairs of escorting Mosquitos, at maximum speed, flew in a shallow dive, opening fire with the four cannons and four machine guns on the destroyer and the minesweepers. The enemy ships, including the U-boat, were putting up a heavy curtain of flak.

Seconds later, Turner started his first diving attack on the U-boat, firing five shots, one of which destroyed one of the guns on the U-boat. Hilliard followed, aiming for the waterline below the conning tower. Turner threw his aircraft into evasive turns, as with full throttle, he climbed into position for a further dive. In all, "L" made four attacks, firing all 24 rounds, and "I" made one.

The *Tsetse* crews were amazed at the rate at which the U-boat was able to turn in its evasive action, but despite the skill of its helmsman, there was no doubt that the U-boat, U-976, had been hit many times, and it was starting to founder.

The fortified Ile d'Yeu was but a short distance away, and its heavy anti-aircraft guns opened fire as the aircraft circled the target area – adding to the hundreds of black puffs filling the sky. This was no place to hang around, once the assault had been completed. Nine minutes from first sighting this naval force, the U-boat had been mortally damaged, the surface ships heavily beaten-up, and the Mosquitos were racing – at sea level – out to sea before turning north for home.

Two days later, On 27th March 1944, these same two *Tsetse* aircraft with the same crews, but this time with an escort of 6 Mosquitos of 248 Squadron, were detailed back to that same part of the Bay of Biscay, and strangely enough at the same time of day. One of the crews of the escorting Mossies was Flt Lt E. H. Jeffreys DFC, and by now Flg Off, A. D. Burden, who had been formally posted into 248 from 618 Squadron on 1st March 1944.

After the excitement and success of the previous run along this mine swept channel, all eyes were extra alert. If there was a U-boat

The Flotilla Commander, La Pallice, inspects the crew of U-960 before its cruise in February 1944. (Günther Heinrich)

*U-960 at sea in 1943. (*Günther Heinrich)

*Armament of U-boat Type VII C, beside the conning tower. (*author)

Torpedo storage in U-995. (Marine-Ehrenmal, Laböe)

Engine room of U-995. (Marine-Ehrenmal, Laböe)

The attack on U-976 begins, the U-boat starting to take evasive action. These photos were taken by the author with a hand-held camera through the aircraft windscreen.

U-976 being hit by a 57mm shell while returning fire. Minesweeper V604 to right. (author)

ABOVE: *Oberleutnant z.S.u Kommandant Raimund Tiesler with other survivors of U-976 ashore at St. Nazaire 25th March 1944.* (Raimund Tiesler)

LEFT: *The Flotilla Commander of the U-boat base, St. Nazaire, welcomes the survivors of U-976.* (Raimund Tiesler)

The Victor *comic in July 1977 printed its version of the attack by Mosquito Mk VXIII 'L' of 618 S.D. (Doug Turner)*

The back page of the Victor *comic. (Doug Turner)*

MARCH 1944.

YEAR 1944		AIRCRAFT		PILOT, OR 1ST PILOT	2ND PILOT, PUPIL OR PASSENGER	DUTY (INCLUDING RESULTS AND REMARKS)
MONTH	DATE	Type	No.			
—	—	—	—	—	—	TOTALS BROUGHT FORWARD
MAR	3	MOSQUITO	HH425	SELF	1 PASSENGER	AIR TO SEA & DOG FIGHT.
MAR	4	MOSQUITO	MM425	SELF.	F/O CURTIS (NAV)	OPS. WITH 248 SHIPPING & SUB PATROL
MAR	5	MOSQUITO	HH425	SELF.	F/O CURTIS (NAV)	DOG FIGHTING & AIR TO SEA
MAR	6	MOSQUITO	HH425	SELF.	F/O CURTIS (NAV)	OPS. SUB PATROL
MAR	7	MOSQUITO	NH425	SELF	F/O CURTIS (NAV)	OPS. SUB PATROL WARNED TRAWLERS MG.
MAR	8	MOSQUITO	HH425	SELF	LAC MITCHELL	TO PREDANNACK & RETURN.
MAR	9	MOSQUITO	MM425	SELF	F/O CURTIS (NAV)	SUB PATROL SUNK 2 SPANISH TRAWLERS MG
MAR	10	MOSQUITO	NM425	SELF	F/O CURTIS (NAV)	SUB PATROL 248. 9 SHOTS AT SUB ACC 4 DES (3. JU.86s DESTROYED 2 PROBAB)
MAR	13	MOSQUITO	HH425	SELF	F/O CURTIS (NAV)	OPS SUB PATROL WITH 157.
MAR	15	MOSQUITO	HH424	SELF	F/O CURTIS (NAV)	OPS ANTI SUB PATROL (NO JOY)
MAR	16	MOSQUITO	DZ700	SELF.	F/O CURTIS (NAV)	A.C. CIRCUS TO NAVAL STATIONS
MAR	18	MOSQUITO	DZ700	SELF	S/L PHILLIPS	TO PORTREATH & RET
MAR	20	MOSQUITO	HH425	SELF	F/O CURTIS (NAV)	OPS. RETURNED COMPASS U/S
MAR	21	MOSQUITO	HH425	SELF	F/O CURTIS (NAV)	OPS. BLEW UP TANKER OFF FRENCH
						COAST ACC BY. H. 248 LOST 1. A/C
MAR	24	MOSQUITO	NH425	SELF	F/O CURTIS (NAV)	OPS. SHIPPING ROVER NO JOY (248)
MAR	24	MOSQUITO	NH425	SELF	CPL THORNTON	C.S. UNIT TEST.
MAR	25	MOSQUITO	HH425	SELF	F/O CURTIS (NAV)	OPS. WITH 248 (LAC) ATTACKED AND
MAR	27	MOSQUITO	HH425			BELIEVE DESTROYED SUBMARINE (SUNK)
MAR	27	MOSQUITO	HH425	SELF	F/O CURTIS (NAV)	OPS. ATTACKED & DAMAGED ONE OF TWO
MAR	28	MOSQUITO	HH425	SELF		SUBS WITH CONVOY OF 11 SHIPS (BIT HOT)
MAR	28	MOSQUITO	NH425	SELF	CPL MARSDEN	TO STONEY CROSS & RETURN.
MAR	31	MOSQUITO	DZ700	SELF	1. PASS	TO HATFIELD & RETURN. VIA FORD
—		—	—	—	—	—

GRAND TOTAL [Cols. (1) to (10)]

656 Hrs. 55 Mins.

TOTALS CARRIED FORWARD

The Log Book of pilot Flg. Off. D. J. Turner recording attacks on 25th and 27th March, 1944.

OPPOSITE PAGE: *The Log Book of navigator Warr Off J. Hoyle recording attacks on 25th and 27th March 1944.* Abbreviations used: R/B Returned to base; St U/C Starboard Undercarriage; JU88' Junkers 88 fighter/bombers; FLAK Anti-aircraft fire; DR Destroyer; M/V Merchant Vessel; coast coastal gun batteries; numbers 26 to 30 the number of operational sorties begun.

Time carried forward :— 37?00 | 70.05

Date	Hour	Aircraft Type and No.	Pilot	Duty	Remarks (including results of bombing, gunnery, exercises, etc.)	Day	Night
21.2.44.	152?	Mosquito E	F/O Hilliard	R/B. Engine Trouble.		.10	
27.2.44.	0725	Mosquito I	F/O Hilliard	08.8/B U/c + weather 26		1.10	
29.2.44.	1205	Mosquito O	F/O Hilliard	St. U/c stuck.		.15	
2.3.44.	1625	Mosquito I	F/O Hilliard	Portreath — Hatfield		1.15	
23.3.44.	1600	Mosquito L	F/O Hilliard	O.P.S. Sea 35'&88' 27		2.00	
25.3.44.	0700	Mosquito I	F/O Hilliard	O.P.S. Escort by 4 Fighter Mosquitos	ATTACK UBOAT but see NO HITS. Reckon F/Turner Pranged it. 28 BAGS OF FLAK FROM 2 ESCORTS 9 DR.	4.05	
27.3.44.	0700	Mosquito I	F/O Hilliard	O.P.S. Escort by 6 Mosquitos.	ATTACK UBOAT 4 CLAIM AT LEAST 4 HITS. INTENSE FLAK FROM 4	4.15	
30.3.44.	1100	Mosquito L	F/O Hilliard	O.P.S. Escort T. by 8 Mosquitos.	ESCORTS, 2 M/V 9 2 subs 9 coast. A/C 29 caught a wallop in nose. NO JOY. LEAD 2 3 0	3.50	

SUMMARY FOR FEBRUARY 9 MARCH

	DAY	NIGHT
OPS	19.00	2.00
NO OPS	2.10	- -
TOTAL	21.10	2.00

D. ?????? Ft. O.C. 618 SQDN DET 248

Total Time: 392.00 | 70.05

around, who would be the first to cry: "Tally Ho"? It matters not who was the first to see the faint outline of ships in the distance. When Doug Turner gave the order to climb, in readiness for an attack, there below, in the morning sun, was a sizeable convoy.

This time the German Navy was taking no chances. There were two U-boats, U-769 and U-960, in line astern, heading for the safety of the coast. Supporting them were four M-class minesweepers, Sperrbrecher 3 of 4,400 tons and Sperrbrecher 175 of 1,400 tons. A sperrbrecher was a merchant ship, of up to 7,000 tons, which had had some of its superstructure removed to make it a floating gun platform – a formidable enemy. The whole convoy opened fire with light and heavy flak, as the Mosquito escorts spread out, before making high-speed runs over the surface ships, raking them with accurate cannon and machine gun fire.

Unfortunately, the VHF and intercom. in Hilliard's "L" had packed in soon after take-off. So he could only hand signal to Turner. Hilliard was the first *Tsetse* to attack – choosing the U-boat at the rear of the convoy, U-960. He saw one of his shells hit the conning tower – but then felt a violent bang, as a shell from the U-boat crashed into the underside of the nose section of his aircraft. The machine gun covers blew open, but as he straightened out, he still had full control of the aircraft.

Turner had started his first dive as Hilliard cleared the target, and, in all, four shells were seen to hit the metalwork. Five other Mosquitos were hit in this attack, one of which, LR363, (Flt Sgt Compton and Sgt Peters) was forced to crash land back at Portreath.

618 Squadron Special Detachment had shown the German Navy that, in spite of the heaviest protection, their U-boats were vulnerable right up to entering the U-boat pens.

More is told about these two attacks, on U-976 and U-960, in the next chapter of this history.

On the last day of that busy month the award was announced of an immediate DSO to Sqn Ldr Tony Phillips in recognition of his gallant leadership during the short time he had been with 618 Squadron Special Detachment.

The sweeps along the mineswept channels onto the Biscay coast during the first ten days of April produced no result. Then, on 11th

April, *Tsetse*s "L" with Hamlett and Mudd, and "I" with Roberts and Winsor, escorted by 5 Mosquitos from 248 Squadron and 6 from 151 Squadron, were ordered onto the Channel C sweep. "L" was forced through mechanical trouble to return to base. Roberts was leading this formation, which was within sight of the land off St. Nazaire, when they saw their targets. There was a U-boat being escorted by a destroyer, a sperrbrecher flak ship, 2 armed trawlers, and circling above them some 8 to 12 JU88's. The sky was alive with flak from all the surface vessels, and an air battle was under way on the fringe of the flak. The fighter Mosquitos pressed home attacks on the escort ships, then turned to engage the JU88's. The enemy did not know at that stage which of the Mosquitos would be going for the U-boat with the dreaded 57 mm field gun. Roberts had seconds only in which to come off the top of his climbing turn, into a high speed dive at his target. He saw splashes from his shells near to the hull of the U-boat but was not able to claim any direct hits. The flak from the U-boat and the ships was worse than anything he had seen on the notorious Dutch coast, when he and Pete Winsor were flying Beaufighters. A cry came over the VHF that the CO of 248 Squadron, Wg Cdr Barron, who had been leading the escorts, had crashed into the sea; almost immediately another of 248's aircraft was shot down.

This had been a costly mission for 248 Squadron – but the extent of the air and sea cover being provided for these U-boats showed how vulnerable the German High Command were feeling.

The next day, Acting Wg Cdr Tony Phillips was posted from 618 Squadron SD to take command of 248 Squadron, with his navigator, Flg Off Tommy Thomson.

On 17th April, during a sweep down the Biscay coastline, the *Tsetse*s and escorts had sighted 8 detroyers.

618 Squadron Special Detachment had made the four attacks that had been called for on 19th October by Coastal Command Headquarters. On 19th April, Tony Phillips, Tommy Thomson, Doug Turner, Des Curtis, Hilly Hilliard and Robbie Roberts were called to HQCC, Northwood, to discuss the *Tsetse* effectiveness against U-boats. There was a need for MAP to tell de Havillands what its longer term requirement for the Mark XVIII would be. Equally, MAP wanted an assessment of the ammunition requirements; a valid

Recent Attacks on U-Boats

On the morning of March 10 **Mosquitos E** and **L/248,** armed with 6-pdr. cannon, were on anti-U-Boat patrol at 100 feet. There was 8/10–9/10 cloud at 1,500 feet and the visibility was 8–10 ·miles. In position 44° 05′ N., 05° 40′ W., they sighted a U-Boat on the surface escorted by four Elbing class destroyers. The force was steering due east at 12 knots. The U-Boat was of the 1,600-type, at least 300 feet long, dark grey in colour and she was armed with four to six guns of various types. Four attacks were made by " E " and one by " L " which formated with " E " during the second run. The U-Boat remained on the surface and she was hit twice on the bows and four or five times near the conning tower. During the first three attacks there was no opposition from the U-Boat and only slight flak from the destroyers. This, however, became intense during the final run. The U-Boat was also escorted· by eight to ten Ju.88s and one of these is claimed as destroyed by " E." Three others were destroyed by Mosquitos from the same squadron which were covering the anti U-Boat aircraft.

Comments

Persistent and determined attacks against a well armed and heavily escorted U-Boat. At least six hits are claimed by these two aircraft with their 6-pounder armament but it is not possible to say what damage or casualties they inflicted. Efforts should be made to obtain photographs of attacks to assist assessment. Otherwise an excellent performance.

COASTAL COMMAND REVIEW Report of U-BOAT ATTACK by 618 Sqn S.D. on 10th MARCH 1944

Coastal Command Review Report of U-boat attacks by 618 Sqn SD on 10th March 1944

On the Enemy's Doorstep

When on anti U-Boat patrol on March 25 in fine but hazy weather with visibility three miles **Mosquitos L** and **I/248,** flying at 50 feet, sighted. a U-Boat on the surface accompanied by two escort vessels, a trawler type ahead and a coaster astern. The position was 46° 48′ N., 02° 43′ W., and the U-Boat, which was dark grey in colour, was steering 030° at 3 knots. The Mosquitos attacked down sun with 6-pdr. cannon, " L " making four runs and " I " one. During the first four attacks intense and accurate flak was put up by the U-Boat and by both escort vessels but during the fifth run only the escorts fired. About ten hits were seen on the conning tower and on the forward deck near and below the waterline. After the attacks the U-Boat submerged and the Navigator of " I " saw an oil patch which he estimated to be 100 yards long and 30 yards wide.

Comments

A determined and very successful series of attacks with excellent confirmatory photographs. The evidence of hits together with the big oil patch seen after the U-Boat disappeared indicates the possibility of serious damage or even foundering.

Two days later the same two Mosquitos and crews were again out on offensive patrol in similar weather. On this occasion they found two U-Boats escorted by eleven vessels, one of which was probably a Sperrbrecher. The convoy was disposed with three A.S.T.s in line abreast followed in line astern by one 4/5,000-ton M/V, two U-Boats and a second M/V. Then came three more A.S.T.s in line abreast with two more astern and to port. There was also one A.S.T. on the U-Boat's starboard beam. The escorts were sighted first and the U-Boats afterwards. The U-Boats looked like 500-tonners and were dark grey in colour with no distinguishing features. Both aircraft attacked the rear U-Boat, " L " on the starboard bow and " I " on the beam. Four hits were seen as well as several possible hits underwater. The U-Boat remained on the surface. Intense heavy and medium flak was put up by all the vessels in the convoy and " I " was damaged.

Comments

A very fine attack indeed pressed home with skill and determination. Evidence states that the U-Boat was hit but it was impossible to stay and observe after results. It must be very depressing for U-Boat crews to realise that they can be shot up on their own front door step even when in company with eleven escorts.

Coastal Command Review Report of U-boat attacks by 618 Sqn SD on 25th and 27th March 1944

COPY — MESSAGE

From: COASTAL COMMAND

To: O.C. 248 SQUADRON.

A.920 26th March 1944.

Please convey my congratulations to all crews engaged in gallant
attack on U Boats and Escorts on 25th March.

SHOLTO DOUGLAS.

A.O.C.-in-C., Coastal Command.

W:.Q^515/P1266 80,000 Pads 10/42 H.P. 51-5588

R.A.F. Form 1924   **POSTAGRAM.**   Originator's Reference Number :—
                                           19G/AOC/S1/2.

   To: R.A.F. Station, Portreath.   Date:— 4th May, 1944.
       (For F/O D. Curtis of No. 248 Squadron).

   From :Headquarters No. 19 Group.   Confidential.

               The Air Officer Commanding and all
       at No. 19 Group most heartily congratulate you
       on your Immediate award of the D.F.C.

Originator's   Wing   Time of
Signature   Commander. Origin

formula was 4 aircraft making 26 sorties a month firing 70% of the 24 rounds carried. An alternative weapon, the RP (Rocket Projectile) was coming into use. This was launched from under-wing rails of a standard Mosquito FB, unlike the dedicated Mark XVIII *Tsetse*.

Shortly afterward, Flg Off's Turner, Curtis and Roberts were awarded DFC's.

On 23rd May 1944, notification came from 18 Group that 618 Squadron Special Detachment was to be disbanded, and the aircraft and crews were to be transferred to 248 Squadron. This made sense, because the original reasons for maintaining a separate identity were no longer valid. The crews could be recalled to 618 Squadron if necessary, but more importantly, the secret nature of the Molins gun had called for segregated maintenance and servicing of the *Tsetse* Mosquitos. This was an uneconomical use of resources, now that the Germans were well aware that some of the attacking Mossies carried 57 mm Kannonen.

So Bonnett, McNicol, Hamlett, Turner, Curtis, Hilliard, Roberts, Hoyle, Mudd and Winsor ended their 14 months' service with The Most Secret Squadron – and it had certainly ended on a high note.

That could be said to complete the 618 Squadron story, but let us stay a little longer with the *Tsetse* weapon, the crews and some other ex-618 types. The 248 Squadron establishment was set at 20 Mark VI FB's and 8 *Tsetse*s as a "C" Flight. The *Tsetse*s were now attacking surface vessels as well as U-boats.

These were hectic days, as the Germans tried to get the remnants of their naval forces into the English Channel which was full of potential targets amongst the invasion craft.

On 7th June, just after D-Day, at 07.29 Turner and Curtis in "L" and Bonnett and McNicol in "O" saw, first, the wash and then a surfacing U-boat, which began to turn violently as the crew rushed to man the guns. The cloud base was too low for the aircraft to get into the ideal 1,500 feet steep dive attack, but each *Tsetse* made a successful first run. But on Bonnett's second run, he must have applied some rudder as the gun jammed. So he made a dummy attack across the target as Turner was coming in for his second run. Hits were seen at the waterline and on the conning tower.

Then the U-boat crash dived, leaving one of the crew outside the vessel. A patch of yellowish brown oil appeared on the surface, but there was insufficient evidence to claim fatal damage. Turner's aircraft was hit in the port wing and engine nacelle. That made Bonnett and McNicol's second U-boat attack and Turner and Curtis their fourth.

The U-boat was U-212, which had just been fitted with a schnorkel and had left La Pallice for a patrol in the English Channel. After repairs she returned to that duty and was sunk by frigates in July.

Two days later, five aircraft of 248 Squadron, led by Wg Cdr Phillips, and including *Tsetses* flown by Turner, Roberts and Bonnett, were detailed to search for survivors of a German destroyer sunk during a battle with Canadian and English destroyers in the English Channel. Off Ile de Batz, on the Britanny coast, some 140 survivors were located in lifeboats and rafts, and Allied naval craft were directed to their rescue. At 17.35 the five aircraft set course for Portreath. Approaching the airfield, Phillips ordered the formation to tighten up, and a pass was made at about 200 feet. Tragedy struck when the formation leader started a climbing turn to starboard to get into the circuit – but he had given no order to "Break away, Break away. Go". Turner, tucked in on the starboard side, put on full throttle and heaved the stick into the pit of his stomach, pulling the Mossie into a vertical climb. Out of danger, he banked and Curtis looked out to see where the others were. Aghast, he saw Bonnett's aircraft severed at the tail, and starting to spiral out of control into the sea. Half a mile away, Phillips' aircraft was flying one wing low, about six feet of outer wing having been sheared off. In turning so quickly, Tony Phillips had left himself no space to get out of the formation.

Al Bonnett and his navigator, Pickles McNicol were probably the most popular crew on the airfield, and this made the accident seem that much sadder. Tony Phillips was completely distraught and haunted by the vision of that collision, despite the efforts of everyone from Gp Capt Somerville, the station commander, and his fellow officers to help him through this grief. On 4th July, a trio of senior officers – Wg Cdr Phillips and Sqn Ldrs Jean Maurice (pseudonym for Max Guedj, Free French Air Force) and Randall went off on a seemingly unimportant patrol over the Brest peninsular. They attacked a small group of minesweepers anchored in Benodet, during which Phillips' aircraft crashed. He and his navigator, Tommy

Thomson, were buried at Benodet. Nothing was said at the time as to why those three senior officers went on that operation; the thoughts of the crews who were close to him that were that Tony had thrown away his own life and that of his navigator.

In a remarkably similar incident early in 1945 at Banff, in Warr Off Bert Mudd, ex 618, flying with Sqn Ldr Gunness and returning from an operation off Norway, were hit by another Mosquito over the airfield. The other crew were killed, but Gunness was able to land SZ959.

There was another occasion of success mixed with sadness, when on the morning of 10th June, a patrol of four 248 Squadron Mossies, led by Stanley Nunn, came across a U-boat close in to Ushant. While the attack was going on, the Mossies were joined by a Liberator, and the U-boat was sunk. That afternoon, a formation led by Max Guedj, DSO, DFC, CdeG, and including 2 *Tsetses*, came across a launch, which opened fire with a light machine gun. The Mossie flown by Flt Lt Jeffries DFC and Flg Off Burden – ex 618 Squadron – was hit and crashed, killing the crew. The combined fire power of the *Tsetses* and escorts destroyed the launch. They were not to know that the launch was carrying the survivors of U-821. Only one German crewman from the U-boat and launch survived.

On 11th July, two *Tsetses*, crewed by Turner and Curtis and Flg Offs Cosman and Freedman, with 16 escorts of 248 Squadron made an evening sortie into the narrow Goulet de Brest, the entrance to this important harbour. A surfaced U-boat was proceeding slowly – with no wake – escorted by three M Class Minesweepers and a sperrbrecher. The shore batteries joined the naval craft in putting up an intense barrage of flak. Cosman made a diving attack on the U-boat, breaking off at 50 yards, and claiming 2 possible hits out of 4 shots fired. At the same time, Turner attacked the sperrbrecher, registering five hits, and creating small explosions on board. Cosman managed to loose off two more 57 mm shells at the leading minesweeper, as the Mosquitos weaved their way through the flak to the mouth of the harbour.

Large formations of Mosquitos and Beaufighters, which were beginning to work as Strike Wings, were now taking on flotillas of ships. For example, 26 aircraft, including Turner and Hoyle, flew into the mouth of the Gironde river to attack a flotilla of minesweepers and a sperrbrecher.

Then in September '44, their work completed on the Biscay coast, the Coastal Command fighter squadrons were moved to Banff (Mosquitos) and Dallachy (Beaufighters), to work as massive Strike Wings against the Germans retreating from Norway. The day after arriving at Banff, Hilliard and Hoyle claimed five hits on a U-boat that their patrol of eight aircraft located off Utvaer.

The last *Tsetse* operational flight was made as part of the Banff Strike Wing on 15th January 1945, when 4 *Tsetse*, with 6 Mk VI FB of 143 Squadron, 4 of 235 Squadron and 2 of the Norwegian 333 Squadron, attacked two flak ships off the South West of Norway. The formation was attacked by 12 FW 190's, and during the engagement, the formation leader, Wg Cdr Max Guedj, and four other crews were lost.

A pilot who served for only a few weeks with 618 Squadron when it was re-formed in July 1944 was Flt Lt T. F. Leaver-Power. He had come from 254 Squadron to which he returned by way of No 132 OTU. 254 and 236 Squadrons, on Beaufighters, made up the North Coates Strike Wing. On 3rd and 4th May 1945, he led the 254 section of a strike force which attacked, on the first day, U-2524, and followed that, on the 4th, with attacks on U-2338, U-2503, U-393 and U-236. The four U-boats either sank or were scuttled in what was to prove the last attacks of the war by that Strike Wing.

The damaged nose panel of Hilly Hilliard's Mosquito (see pages 182-3 for description).

CHAPTER 10

Warriors Above and Below the Sea Meet

618 Squadron had been formed to carry out a highly dangerous mission, which was not consummated. It reformed to take part in the final defeat of the Japanese, but did not make one operational mission. As one of those who was with the squadron from its formation to its disbandment at Narromine, Leon Murray, so aptly puts it:–

"To take part in one big non-event is bad enough, but to take part in two smacks of carelessness!"

But the activities of its Special Detachment demonstrated very clearly that, with the correct weapon, those hand-picked crews – in that superb aircraft – were capable of dealing heavy blows on the enemy.

In all, 94 pilots and navigators served with 618 Squadron and its Special Detachment; their names are recorded in Appendix i. It has not been possible to trace all the details on each of them, such as the units from which they came or to where they were posted on leaving the squadron. The list of decorations earned by these men may also be incomplete, but even as it stands it is most impressive. Most had been decorated for acts of bravery before joining the squadron. In the seven months in which the small Tsetse Special Detachment operated, one DSO and three DFC's were awarded.

It is to be hoped that no additions need to be made to the notation of those who lost their lives while serving with the Royal and Common-wealth Air Forces.

After the war, the survivors got down to the task of creating or re-creating a peaceful life, and reflections on those hectic and sometimes dangerous years were kept as private thoughts. "Living for tomorrow" was a more popular catch phrase than "what did you do in the war?'' But as these veterans moved towards the end of their working lives, there was more time to talk and reminisce. Reunions became more popular – not to celebrate or glorify war, but for the pleasure of meeting again people with whom untold experiences had been shared. The stories were also beginning to hold some interest for the newer generations.

A sequence of events culminated in some unexpected meetings. In 1979 Des Curtis was persuaded by his wife, Margaret, to commission a painting of the *Tsetse* Mossies attacking the U-boat on 25th March 1944. The aviation artist, P. Westacott, was a Metropolitan Police officer working at Hendon. He researched the attack in the archives at the nearby RAF Museum where he learned that the U-boat was numbered U-976.

In 1981 the crew of Hilly Hilliard and Jimmy Hoyle met up again for the first time since the war.

In 1984 Roy Conyers Nesbit wrote a book, ''The Strike Wings'', in which brief reference was made to the attack on U-976. Des Curtis and Hilly Hilliard, independently, made contact with Roy Nesbit, as a result of which they learned the name of the U-boat archivist, Herr Horst Bredow in Cuxhaven. Hilly also got in touch with Des.

They were both interested to know the fate of the crews of the two U-boats that had been attacked on 25th and 27th March. Hilly wrote to Herr Bredow to enquire about U-960, and Des about U-976. German law prevented the authorities from revealing directly to Allied enquirers the present whereabouts of former servicemen. Herr Horst confirmed that the captains of the U-boats were both alive, and he offered to forward any non-offensive mail to either of them.

Writing a letter to a person whom you have not met face to face, but whom you passed at 370 mph as you tried to shoot his ship from under him, and who may not understand English, is not the easiest task.

Early in 1988, Hilly Hilliard wrote, via Horst Bredow, to Gunther 'Heini' Heinrich, the commander of U-960 attacked on 27th March, in which he said that, in the course of the attack, Hilly's Mosquito had been hit in the nose. Gunther Heinrich wrote back, in March, from his home on the riverside north of Hamburg:–

"If you still have the damaged nose panel of your Mosquito I have two scars just over my left knee where a piece of the shell you fired hurts me. That shell wounded three sailors of U-960, one heavily." What a splendid piece of repartee with which to open. He went on to briefly describe how their U-boat was sunk on 19th May 1944 in the Mediterranean, after a prolonged attack by RAF aircraft and four US destroyers. Only 20 of the 51 man crew survived, and the diminishing numbers of survivors meet on the anniversary of the loss at the U-boat Memorial at Möltenort, north of Kiel.

Heini Henrich concluded his letter: "I and also the other members of the U-boat crew are very pleased to hear of you and it would give us also a great pleasure and honour to meet you brave hunter. It would be a great favour to bid welcome to you in Hamburg". Hilly and one of his sons flew to Hamburg to meet Heini Heinrich, and to be with the survivors during the 1989 reunion. A firm bond of friendship had been established.

In December 1989 Des Curtis wrote from Wimborne to the former captain of U-976, Herr Raimund Tiesler:–

"I do not write German; therefore I must hope that your knowledge of English is good.

"We came into conflict on 25th March 1944 when you were in command of Unterseeboote U-976. I was the leading navigator of the formation of six Mosquito aircraft which attacked your submarine, off the French port of St. Nazaire.

"Two of the Mosquito aircraft, including the one I was flying in, were equipped with a 57 mm artillery gun which could fire 24 times. The other four aircraft were our fighter escorts, with 20 mm cannons.

"Earlier this year I met, for the first time since October 1944, the pilot of the other Mosquito with the 57 mm gun. The same two aircraft were flying in the same part of the Bay of Biscay on 27th March when we discovered U-960. In that attack 14 crewmen of U-960 were injured, and our Number 2 Mosquito was hit. The pilot, Mr Hilliard, has been to Hamburg this year to meet Herr Gunther Heinrich, who was in command of U-960. Mr Hilliard gave me your name and said that you were now living in Westfalen.

"Herr Horst Bredow, the U-Boot-Archiv, has kindly agreed to send this letter to you. I am hoping that you will wish to reply to me in due course either directly or through Herr Bredow. I will be sending him next year some information such as the copies of my flying record, or log book."

Ten days later, Raimund Tiesler replied from his home in Herdecke:–

"Many thanks for your letter of Dec 10th. Of course I was surprised when Mr. Bredow called me for my agreement to give my address to you. Now it seems a miracle that we get contact more than 45 years after our fight. How did you learn the number of my submarine at that time? Indeed there arise lots of questions.

"Today it's impossible to touch all that. I'm busy with preparations for the holidays, sorry. But I hope we may continue in January. If possible I would visit you in Wimborne. This name reminds (me of) my stay in Bournemouth for a fortnight in 1967 when I lived in Wimborne Road. I'll write again later."

Obviously the only way to start to find the answers to those questions would be to meet. But Raimund Tiesler was suffering the continuing effects of wounds to his hips inflicted during the raid on St Nazaire harbour in March 1942. The two men continued to correspond, often while Raimund was in hospital enduring one operation after another, or, for some months, without one hip joint. Then in March 1993 he wrote to say that he had been discharged from hospital, and hoped to be sufficiently recovered to receive a visit from the Curtis' in early summer.

On a warm summer's afternoon, Margaret and Des Curtis drove into the delightful small town of Herdecke, in the Ruhr valley. The road on which the Tieslers lived was steep, with equally steep driveways. With a strange feeling of nervousness and perhaps that he was in some way intruding, Des went first into the garden at the rear of the house. At a garden table was a white haired man, who, hearing Des call: "I am looking for Herr Tiesler", picked up two walking sticks and stood to greet his former enemy.

It was not a situation in which to make that upper-lip Englishism: "How do you do". Emotion decided how they should greet each other – by a long close hug, then, looking to see whether the favourable impressions that were coming through in the correspondence were borne out. Des saw a kind, gentle face, drawn by the long years of agony from his illness. Raimund said that he looked into Des' eyes and 'liked what he saw'. Margaret was relieved that what she had dreaded – that one would take an instant dislike to the other – was not going to happen. Frau Ilse Tiesler, who likewise had decided to witness the meeting from a discreet distance, sighed with relief at what she observed.

Documents and pictures were soon produced. Raimund Tiesler had a copy of the ship's log of that day in March, (see Appendix iv).

Raimund Tiesler and Des Curtis meet in Herdecke, Ruhr, in June 1993.
(author)

OPPOSITE PAGE, TOP: *Hilly Hilliard and Günther Heinrich (Commander of U-960) enjoy a beer at Laböe, May 1989.* (Hilly Hilliard)

OPPOSITE PAGE, BOTTOM: *Hilly Hilliard and Des Curtis talk over old times in April 1990.* (Bournemouth Evening Echo)

ABOVE: *Raimund Tiesler and Des Curtis lowering the Union Flag at sundown, Herdecke, Ruhr, in June 1993.* (author)

LEFT: *Commandant Heinrich.*

Doug Turner, Des Curtis, Raimund Tiesler and Hilly Hilliard at the author's home in May 1994. (author)

The wreck of U-976 lying in 60 metres off Ile de Noirmoutier, France. (GREM Nantes)

The German Navy used codes to denote entrances to mineswept channels – in this instance, 439 Herz. In the heat of the battle, the U-boat crew believed that they were being attacked by four-engined aircraft; in fact, only Mosquitoes were involved but the Tsetses were carrying drop tanks outboard of each engine, and the drop tank extended slightly forward of the leading edge, which could suggest additional engines.

Herr Tiesler had invited the Westfalen Post paper to record this historic meeting. While they were taking photographs, the reporter asked for a description of the battle. Des Curtis then handed Raimund Tiesler a photograph of the painting, together with the signatures of the four Tsetse crew members who took part in the attack.

In one of Raimund's books, in addition to the sinking of U-976, there was a brief account of an attack by Flg Off A. L. Bonnett on U-123, which was commanded by an old friend of Raimund, Oberleutnant (later Admiral) von Schroeter. Des recounted the circumstances in which Al Bonnett later lost his life, and how he, Des, had been able to fill in a lot of detail for Al Bonnett's relatives in British Columbia.

The town of Herdecke lay in the path of the flood-waters that were released when the wall of the Möhne dam was breached during the raid by 617 Squadron in the early hours of 17th May 1943. A paper-mill recorded flood water more than 14 feet above the highest recorded water level. One of the supports of the long and high viaduct carrying the main railway from Dortmund was destroyed, leaving the track suspended between the arches. The four new friends went to the Möhne dam, and Raimund was surprised to learn that Des had taken part in the trials of the 'bouncing bomb' as a marine weapon.

Those two full days at Herdecke brought together two men who, as young men, had sought to kill each other. The easy flow of conversation contained no suggestion of recrimination or acccusation. Both considered that war and the destruction of life and property was the most negative display of human intelligence. There were many more fruitful topics on which this new-found friendship was being built.

From Herdecke the Curtis' journeyed up to Hamburg. Over dinner with former business associate, Herr Wilhelm and Frau Ise von Ilsemann, the sad story was told of how Ise's father, General Carl-

Heinrich von Stûlpnagel, a conspirator in the attempt on Hitler's life in July 1944, attempted suicide while under escort back from France to Berlin, and then was summarily executed. His wife and daughter, Ise, were imprisoned in a Gestapo prison by the SS. This was another aspect of how a young person's life was tragically affected in war.

The von Ilsemanns wanted to know all about the meeting in Herdecke. After dinner, Des telephoned the former commander of U-960, Gunther Heinrich, at Blankenesee, who was able to travel with Margaret and Des to Labe the next day.

So, a second meeting of former enemies took place – and, as with the visit earlier of Hilly Hilliard, 'Heini' Heinrich gave them a tour of a Mark VIIC U-boat, U-995, which is now a museum piece. This was the same size of U-boat as U-976 and U-960. Overall length 67 metres, maximum width 6.20 m, she was home to 51 men during a six-week patrol, they sharing the limited space with 12 torpedos, ammunition for the guns, diesel fuel and food. With neither space for a shower nor water for a head-to-toe wash, Heini remarked that he knew who was passing his minute bunk by their smell!

Overlooking the U-boat and the bay of Kiel is a massive memorial to all German sailors. Below decks, in a large cavern, the eternal flame burns. There were wreaths from the Royal British Legion and the Royal Naval Association.

A few kilometres away, at Möltenort, are the sombre rough-hewn stone walls on which have been mounted cast bronze plaques listing, by ship, the names of all those who have died in German submarines in the two World Wars. Knowing that, in the Second World War, the German submarine service suffered the greatest percentage of casualties than any other service of all nations, the list of names on those plaques seemed endless. Heini showed the names of the twenty members of his crew who were lost in the Mediterranean. One of the shortest lists was that of U-976 – thank God.

Hilly Hilliard and Des Curtis have both made the journey to this memorial to pay their respects to those who lost their lives in that brief battle. To these RAF aircrew, those men were faceless – unlike the memories of their colleagues on the squadron, who gave their young lives during those same years of war.

On 7th May 1994 the former commander of U-976, while staying with his wife at the author's home in Dorset, met pilots, Doug Turner and Hilly Hilliard, and their wives. That was, also, the first time that these two pilots had met since January 1945.

That these men who fought their wars over the sea and under the sea should meet nearly half a century later and make firm friendships is a fitting epilogue to this story.

As if to complete the story, Raimund Tiesler received from the French "Groupe de recherches et d'exploration maritime" a photograph of U-976 lying in some 60 metres of water about 35 nautical miles from St. Nazaire harbour. The Frenchmen were surprised that Herr Tiesler was able to put them in touch with one of those who sank that U-boat. This French team then contacted the author, seeking material for inclusion in a report. Three of them travelled to Laböe, where they met Herr Tiesler and three other former crew members of the submarine. Later, on 25th March 1995 – 51 years to the day of the attack on U-976 – they came to England to be taken by the author to the Mosquito Museum, where they filmed the Molins guns, and a Mosquito. It is intended that, at the time of the celebrations of the 50th Anniversary of VE-Day, the author, the four U-boat crew and the French divers will meet at St Nazaire. Doubtless, the older men will be reminiscing; their memories will not be of gladiatorial victory or defeat, but of the loss of comrades.

No 618 Squadron had a short but remarkable existence. It is difficult to imagine the confusion that might have reigned if the *Tirpitz* had silently moved anchorage to Trondheim in the summer of 1943 while the performance problems of the *Highball* weapon were still being encountered, and the squadron had not been able to put its full complement of Mosquitos into the air at any one time. But, to use the phraseology of the Commander-in-Chief, Coastal Command, this was not 'any old squadron with its usual ration of Pilot Officer Prunes;' each of the aircrew was prepared to give his all in meeting the enormous task for which he had been selected.

THE BADGE OF U-BOAT U-976

A Shield with this Badge was presented by the former Commander of U-976 to each of the four Mosquito aircrew of No 618 Squadron who attacked the U-boat on 25th March 1944

APPENDIX I

Aircrew who served with No 618 Squadron

NAME and Initials	RANK	AWARDS	FROM	DIED	TO
BAKER D J	Flt Lt		236		INDIA
BELCHER W R M	Flt Lt		248		INDIA
BELL E	Flg Off		544	KILLED	19/6/45 AUSTRALIA
BINKS A F	Sqn Ldr	DFC	235		INDIA
BLAKE J B	Warr Off		27		254 Sqdn
BOLGER D G	Flg Off		254		INDIA
BONNETT* A L RCAF	Flg Off		236	KILLED	9/6/44 at PORTREATH
BOREHAM F B	Flg Off				Last Man at Narromine
BROWN* G R	Flg Off		139		INDIA
BURDEN* 458 D R	Warr Off		236		BECCLES
BURDEN* 968 D A	Flg Off		143	KILLED	10/6/44 on 248 Sqdn
BURROWS			544		
CARON	Flt Sgt			MISSING	21/2/44 on 143 Sqdn
CAWKER H R	Flg Off		544		
CLUTTERBUCK T M	Flt Lt	DFC	540		
COBBLEDICK L T	Flt Lt		248		INDIA
COWLEY	Flt Sgt			KILLED	4/11/43 on 618SD, Cornwall
CURTIS* D	Flt Lt	DFC	235		248 Sqdn
CUSSENS* A S	Flt Lt		105		SCULTHORPE
D'ALTON E	Flg Off		254		132 OTU
DONALD* R W	Flg Off		139		INDIA
ELLIS* K H N	Flg Off		139		INDIA
EMBREY* W RCAF	Flt Lt		139		8/8/44 to CANADA
EMERY W J	Flg Off				279 Sqdn
FLETCHER* R C	Flg Off	DFM	139		INDIA
FOSS* F S	Flt Lt		235	KILLED	BRUNEI
FRENCH F	Flt Lt		235	KILLED	27/7/45 AUSTRALIA

GARDNER	Warr Off		235		INDIA
GERRARD W G	Flt Lt		143		INDIA
GOODMAN G E	Flt Lt		East Fortune		119 Sqdn
GROOME* J G	Flt Lt		235		INDIA
HALLEY*			105		
HAMLETT* K	Flt Lt		235		248 Sqdn
HAMMOND			235		
HILLIARD* A H	Flt Lt		235		248 Sqdn
HOPWOOD* H C	Flt Lt		105		INDIA
HOYLE* J B	Warr Off		235		248 Sqdn
HUTCHINSON* G H B	Gp Capt	DFC	235		INDIA
INSKEEP J D	Flg Off		540		INDIA
JACK J C	Flg Off		540		INDIA
JACKSON*	Flt Sgt		521		
JEFFREYS* E H	Flt Lt	DFC	143	KILLED	10/6/44 on 248 Sqdn
KNIGHT			6 OTU		
LAWTON V	Flt Lt		235		INDIA
LEAVER-POWER T F	Flt lt		254		132 OTU
MACLEAN I	Flg Off			KILLED	By sniper JAKARTA
MADDOCKS D G	Flg Off	DFC			INDIA
MAKINS*	Flt Lt	DFC	105		SCULTHORPE
MASSEY* J	Flg Off	DFM	139	KILLED	road accident SINGAPORE
MATTHEWS D S	Flg Off				INDIA
MAYNARD G L	Flt Lt				repat to UK 1945
McREADY* H B	Flt Lt		139		
McGOLDRICK J S RAAF	Sqn Ldr		540	KILLED	27/7/45 AUSTRALIA
McNICHOL McD	Flg Off			KILLED	9/6/44 on 248 Sqdn
MELVILLE-JACKSON* G M	Sqn Ldr	DFC	248		INDIA
MILNE A R W	Warr Off		235	KILLED	11/10/44 in E. YORKS
MORRIS	Flt Sgt		236		
MUDD* A	Warr Off		235		248 Sqdn
MUNRO A W	Flt Sgt		105		SCULTHORPE
MURRAY J McK	Flg Off		144		INDIA
MURRAY* L	Flg Off		105		INDIA
MYLES RCAF	Plt Off	DFC	544		
OAKLEY A L	Flg Off	DFC	254		INDIA
PALMER B J	Flt Sgt				BECCLES
PAVEY* D L	Flg Off		105	KILLED	5/4/43 at SKITTEN
PENFOLD			236		

Name	Rank	Awards	Sqdn	Fate	TO
PHILLIPS A L	Wg Cdr	DSO, DFC	248	KILLED	4/7/44 on 248 Sqdn
POLLARD	Flt Sgt			MISSING	21/2/44 on 143 Sqdn
PRICE J E	Flt Lt		143		INDIA
RENNIE* G W RCAF	Flt Lt		139		CANADA on repat
ROBERTS* B C	Flt lt	DFC	248	KILLED	22/2/45 on 248 Sqdn
ROCHFORD	Flt lt	540		KILLED	2/5/45 at MASCOT
ROSE C F	Sqn Ldr	DFC, DFM	521	KILLED	4/11/43/ on 618SD, Cornwall
SAVAGE			236		
SCARGILL M C	Flt lt	DFC	236		4/45 repat to UK
SILLITO E B	Flt Lt	DFC	540	KILLED	19/6/45 AUSTRALIA
STACEY	Warr Off		236		INDIA
STEPHEN* D A	Flt lt		105		INDIA
STIMSON*	Sgt		105	KILLED	5/4/43 at SKITTEN
STRANGE E V B	Flt Lt				INDIA
STUBBS E A	Flt Sgt		235	KILLED	11/10/44 in E YORKS
TEMPLETON* F	Flg Off		139		INDIA
THOMAS E H	Flt Lt	DFC			INDIA
THOMSON R W	Flg Off	DFC	248	KILLED	4/7/44 on 248 Sqdn
THORBURN* G G P	Flg Off		105		INDIA
TURNER* D J	Flt Lt	DFC	235		248 Sqdn
TURTON R C	Flg Off	DFC			INDIA
UMBERS* A	Flg Off		248		INDIA
WALKER* J	Flg Off		105		INDIA
WALTERS S I	Flt Lt	DFC	235		INDIA
WATKINS V C	Flg Off		144		INDIA
WESTON* F J RNZAF	Flt Lt		139		INDIA
WICKHAM* A T	Flt Lt	DFC	105		SCULTHORPE
WINSOR* F G	Warr Off		248	KILLED	22/2/45 on 248 Sqdn

*Denotes an Original Member on formation of the squadron

The Rank shown is the last known rank

The column 'TO' shows the official posting from the squadron

APPENDIX II

New Crews posted in on re-formation of Squadron

On 11th July 1944 the following inward postings were promulgated:–

From 143 Squadron: Flg Off Gerrard & Flg Off Price
From 144 Squadron: Flg Off J McK Murray & Flt Sgt VC Watkins
From 235 Squadron: Flt Lt Hammond & Warr Off Gardner, Warr Off Milne & Flt Sgt Stubbs
From 236 Squadron: Flt Lt MC Scargill & Flg Offs DJ Baker and Penfold & Flt Sgt Savage, Warr Off Stacey & Flt Sgt Morris
From 248 Squadron: Flt Lt Cobbledick & Flg Off WRM Belcher
From 254 Squadron: Flg Offs Oakley & Bolger, Flt Lt T F Leaver-Power & Flg Off E D'Alton; (the latter crew were posted to 132 OTU on 4th August.)

The Photo Reconnaissance crews were:–

From 540 Squadron: Flt Lt's McGoldrick, R.A.A.F. Clutterbuck, & Rochford, Flg Off Sillito, Plt Off Jack and Flt Sgt Inskeep
From 544 Squadron: Flg Off HR Cawker & Flt Sgt Burrows, Plt Off E Bell & Plt Off Myles, DFC, RCAF

APPENDIX III

Extract from the Log of U-976

24.03.44

0310 ß 0309/24/10 Stehe 30 Std. vor Einlaufhafen.
0910 FT: 0446/24/15 : Geleit steht 25.03.
0900 Punkt 439 Herz.

25.03.44

0300 Augetaucht auf dem Außenweg.
0700 ONO 2, See , Sicht 2 sm
     Funktionnshießen der Fla.Waffen.
0758 FrÜhdienst. Treffpunkt mit Geleit erreicht. Da Geleit noch nicht
     in Sicht, 8 sm abgelaufen und wieder zuruckgelaufen.
0900 Geleitfahrzeuge kommen in Sicht.
0903 6 Flugzeuge, als "He 177" angesprochen, im Vorbeiflug
     E = 4000m. Höhe 20m.
0910 Vom Geleit aufgenommen. "VP604" setzt sich vor, "VP 448"
     schert ins Kielwasser ein.
0915 "VP 604" setzt "Flieger" .
0920 6 Flugzeuge im Vorbeiflug an Bb.
0922 Angriff von Stb. Typ "Moskito", Feuererlaubniss Flugzeug
     greift nur mit schweren Bordwaffen an. Auf der Brucke ein
     Toter mehrere Verwundete an den 2 cm Waffen. Bb.Zwilling
     zerschossen. Weitere Angriffe von Stb. aus der Aonne nun auch
     von 4-mot. Maschinen.
     Nach dem 3. Anflug Flak 3,7 Vollautomatisch ausgefallen. Es
     wird einzeln mit Hand weitergeladen. Boot wird stark
     achterlastig. Ich nehme Treffer in Tauchzelle 1 an und gebe
     Befehl Tauchbunker 2 auszudrucken, gleich darauf sämtliche
     Tauchbunker ausdruckeen, Flutklappen schließen.

0930 Vom L.I. Meldung: "Wassereinbruch Kombuse". Etwas später, Boot läßt sich nicht mehr halten. Ich gebe Befehl: "Alle Mann aus dem Boot."

Das Boot wurde geräumt, die Verwundeten wurden zuletzt vom L.I. Lt. (Ing.) Gneuß, und Zentralmaat Masch.Mt. Reckordt auf die Brucke geschafft. Inzwischen erfolgten weitere Anfluge von 4mot. Maschinen. Sie greifen meist in Gruppen zu 2-4 Maschinen an und setzen nur schwere Brodwaffen ein. Nach dem5. Anflug vollstÄnddiger Ausfall der 3,7 cm. Schuß fÄllt nicht, trotzdem Verschluß verriegelt. Ein Teil der Besatzung, die aus dem Boot kommt geht ans Oberdeck zunÄchst in Deckung vom Turm.

Die Stb.Zwilling schießt nun allein weiter unter der kaltblutigen Bedienung des Mtr.Ob.Gefr. Rosin. Es erfolgten noch 3 Anfluge. 2 Anfluge kamen von Stb. einer von Bb.Das Boot ist inzwischen stark achterlastig geworden und hat Schlagseite nach Stb. Etwa 30 mann. die nicht hinter dem Turm stehen, werden vom Wasser steuerbords gespuhlt. Der rest befindet sich auf der Brucke und Vorschiff. Beide Diesel laufen H.F. weiter. Um das Boot noch steuerfÄhig zu halten, steigt der II.WO Ob. FÄhnr. Borchert noch einmal in den Turm und fuhrt die Rudebefehle aus. Er verharrt dort bis zur letzten Minute, bis er von mir hochgerufen wird.

Das Boot kommt noch einmal achtern hoch, fängt dann jedoch an wieder stark achterlastig zu werden und sinkt uber den Achtersteven ab. 0940. Es sinkt unter drei Hurras, die der I.WO Lt.z.S. Hinrichs, der als letzter auf der Brucke stand, auf das sinkende Boot ausbrachte. Die Flugzeuge haben die starke Achterlastigkeit des Boots wohl beobachtet, sind jedoch noch vor dem Sinken abgeflogen und außer Sicht gekommen.

Die zwei Gruppen der Besatzung wurden von den VP-Bootenaufgenommen. Es wirkte sich gunstig aus, daß die Leute jeweils in zwei Gruppen dicht beisammen waren. Ein Uffz. ist auf der Brucke gefallen. 2 Uffz. und 1 Mann wurden bei deen letzten Angriffen auf dem Vorschiff tdlich getroffen. Davon wurde 1 Uffz. und 1 Mann spÄter noch geborgen.

Der tatgräftigen und kameradschaftlichen Hilfe einzelner Soldaten ist es zu verdanken, daß alle Verwundeten, darunter 3 Schwerverwundete, in ihrem hilflosen Zustandd geborgeb werden konnten. Die Bergung von Seiten der VP – Boote war nach etwa 30 min. beendet.

Die Besatzung zeigte in diesem Gefecht Ruhe und Kaltblutigkeit. Der Befehl "all Mann aus dem Boot" wurde ruhig augefuhrt. Ganz besonders haben sich die Bedienungen des Stb. 2 cm Zwillings hervorgetan. Die Bedienung musste einige Male wegen Ausfall durch Verwundung wechseln.

Zu dem Angriff ist zu bemerken : Die Angriffe der Fluzgeuge erfolgen fast stets aus der Sonne, in Gruppen zu 2-4 Maschinen. Meist waren es 4-mot.Flugzeuge, die im steilen Gleitflug auf das Boot flogen und mit allen Kailbern ihre Bordwaffen schossen. Die verwendeten Kaliber waren etwa 7 mm, 17 mm und 4 cm. Bomben oder Raketen habe ich nicht beobachtet. Der Flakschutz durch die beiden VP-Boote war nicht ausreichend bei der Anzahl und StÄrke der Maschinen.

Die eigene Flak 3,7 cm lag gut bei den Flugzeugen bis aif einne Rauchfahne bei einem Flugzeug konnten keine wirkungsvollen Treffer beobachtet werden. Durch den Ausfall des Bb. Zwillings und spÄteren Strung an der Flak 3,7 cm wurde die Abwehr des Bootes wesentlich geschwÄcht.

Der Verlust des Bootes ist auf den starken Wassereinbruch in der Kombuse und Battr.-Selbstschalterraum zuruckzufuhren. Außerdem waren Tauchzelle 1 und Tauchbunker 2 Stb. und Backboard mit Sicherheit und Tauchzelle 5 wahrscheinlich durchschossen.

Tiesler
Oberleutnant z.S. u. Kommandant.

APPENDIX IV

Translation of Extract from Log of U-976

Translation by courtesy of Herr K. Feddersen

24.03.44

0310 SS 0309/24/10 30 hours out from base.
0910 Wireless message 0446/24/15 Convoy positioning 25.03 (next day) at 0900 hours at Position 439 Heart (codename)

25.03.44

0300 Surfaced at outer edge of (mineswept) lane.
0700 Course East-North-East. Sea state 1, Visibility 2 n.ms. Testing anti-aircraft guns.
0758 First day shift. Reached convoy rendez-vous point. Convoy not sighted, so sail 8 n.ms along and back through the channel.
0900 Convoy sighted
0903 6 aircraft (wrongly) identified as HE 177's, pass at range of 4,000 metres, height 20 m.
0910 Joined convoy. Escort Vessel VP 604 leading, VP 448 bringing up the rear.
0915 Escort Vessel VP 604 makes flag signal: "Hostile aircraft"
0920 6 aircraft sighted to port.
0921 First attack from starboard by Mosquitos. Permission to gun crews to open fire. Aircraft firing only heavy cannon. One dead on the bridge, several wounded manning the 2 cm gun. Port side twin-gun destroyed. More attacks out of the sun by 4-engined aircraft. After 3 attacks the automatic loading of the 3,7 cm

anti-aircraft gun was out of action, so re-loading had to be done manually. Boat becoming heavy to control. I assume we are hit in Tank 1, and order Tank 2 to be emptied, then all tanks to be emptied. Valves closed.

0930 Chief Engineer reports water coming into the galley; a little later, that boat cannot be saved. I give the order: "Abandon ship".

The boat was cleared, the wounded were hoisted to the bridge by Eng. Lt. Gneuss and Leading Artificer Reckordt. Meantime, more attacks by 4-engined aircraft. They usually attack in groups of 2 to 4 aircraft, and only fire heavy weapons.

After the 5th attack, the 3,7 cm gun completely out of action although the breach was loaded. Some of the crew who were trying to abandon ship take cover behind the conning tower. The starboard twin-gun, coolly operated by Leading Seaman Rosin, is now the only gun in action. Three further attacks, two from starboard and one from port. About 30 sailors, not protected by the conning tower, are washed overboard on the starboard side. The rest are on the bridge and on the fo'c'sle.

Both engines are still running at half speed. To keep the boat maneuverable, Sub Lieut. Borchert re-enters the tower and carries out steering orders. He stays there until the last minute – until called up on deck by me.

The boat comes up slightly but then gets heavier aft and begins to sink by the stern.

0940 The boat sinks. "Three cheers" are led by the Navigating Officer Hinrichs, the last man on the bridge.

The aircraft must have seen the heavy list of the boat, but they left and were out of sight before the boat sank.

The two groups of the crew were taken on board the escort vessels. It was fortuitous that the men were in two groups and close together. One petty officer was killed on the bridge. Two petty officers and one seaman were fatally wounded during one of the last attacks against the stern of the boat. The bodies of one petty officer and one seaman were later recovered.

Due to the energetic and comradely help of some soldiers, all the wounded, including three very seriously injured, were rescued. The rescue operation by the escort vessels was completed in about 30 minutes.

During this engagement, the crew displayed calm and resolve.

The order to abandon ship was obeyed calmly. The gun crews, manning the starboard 2 cm twin-gun, distinguished themselves particularly. Several times gunners had to be replaced through injury.

The following can be added to the attack report:–

The aircraft almost always attacked out of the sun in groups of 2 to 4 aircraft. They were mostly four-engined, diving steeply; the boat opend up with all available weapons. Calibre sizes were 7 mm, 17 mm and 40 mm. I did not see any bombs or rockets. The anti-aircraft capability of the two U-boats was insufficient against the numbers and strength of the aircraft.

The fire from our own 37 mm flak covered the aircraft well, but apart from one trail of smoke from one aircraft, no other hits could be detected.

The boat's capability to defend itself was considerably lessened by the loss of the port twin-gun and the subsequent defects of the 37 mm flak gun.

The loss of the boat can be attributed to the large intake of water into the galley and the battery room. In addition, Tanks 1 and 2, port and starboard, were definitely hit, and in all probability Tank 5.

Tiesler
Oberleutnant z.S. u. Kommandant

8th May 1995 over the wreck in the Bay of Biscay off St Nazaire (left to right), the author, Lt.z.S. Hindrichs, Lt. (Ing.) Gneuß, Oberleutnant z.S.u Kommandant Tiesler, Unteroff Zentrale Ellingbaus, of U-976 and in the wheelhouse, M. Maurice Grenon, French diver who found U-976.

Index